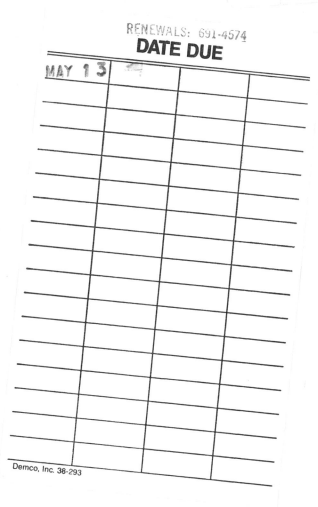

SOFTWARE MAINTENANCE GUIDEBOOK

Robert L. Glass books published by Prentice-Hall

SOFTWARE RELIABILITY GUIDEBOOK

SOFTWARE MAINTENANCE GUIDEBOOK

Robert L. Glass
Ronald A. Noiseux

PRENTICE-HALL, INC.
Englewood Cliffs, New Jersey 07643

Library of Congress Cataloging in Publication Data

GLASS, ROBERT L   date
    Software maintenance guidebook.

    Bibliography: p.
    Includes index.
    1. Electronic digital computers—Programming.
I. Noiseux, Ronald A., joint author.   II. Title.
QA76.6.G56   001.64′2   80-21967
ISBN: 0-13-821728-9

Printed in the United States of America

10 9 8 7 6 5 4 3 2 1

Editorial Production/Supervision by Theodore Pastrick
Manufacturing buyer: Joyce Levatino

PRENTICE-HALL INTERNATIONAL, INC., *London*
PRENTICE-HALL OF AUSTRALIA PTY. LIMITED, *Sydney*
PRENTICE-HALL OF CANADA, LTD., *Toronto*
PRENTICE-HALL OF INDIA PRIVATE LIMITED, *New Delhi*
PRENTICE-HALL OF JAPAN, INC., *Tokyo*
PRENTICE-HALL OF SOUTHEAST ASIA PTE. LTD., *Singapore*
WHITEHALL BOOKS LIMITED, *Wellington, New Zealand*

CONTENTS

v

PREFACE

Maintenance is the enigma of software:
Enormous amounts of dollars are spent on it.
Little research or management attention is given to it.
And, in fact, it is not even a well-defined concept!

The time has come to begin removing the shroud of Merlinism which surrounds maintenance. This book is an attempt to do just that.

It begins by placing maintenance into the perspective of the "software life cycle" concept, and presents a definition of the term "maintenance."

It moves then to an unusual point of view — the importance of people in software maintenance. The theme is developed that the maintainer is an unsung hero, quietly keeping the computer software products humming in a world where little attention and few accolades are handed out.

With this people-oriented foundation, the book then moves to the meat of the subject — what technologies, both old and new, can be used by these unsung heroes? Tools and techniques which the maintainer should know about are described, ranging from the mundane (code reformatters) to the blue sky (the supercompiler). Heavy emphasis is put on the up-front activity of doing it right the first time — methods by which the software developer can ease the problems of the software maintainer. A liberal number of examples is presented, most coded in the newly-emerging Department of Defense programming language Ada.

As a non-identical twin to the technologist point of view, the book then provides a management perspective on maintenance. Planning, organizing, and directing maintenance are all discussed. A somewhat radical view of software documentation is presented — one which has enormous promise for improved documentation quality, but one which requires new management thinking.

And finally, to bring the subject into focus and add a touch of reality, a maintainer's diary is presented — a day-to-day documenting of some of the events which characterize the software maintainer's on-the-job lifestyle.

Sprinkled throughout is a nearly complete bibliography of references to software maintenance in the literature. Symptomatic of the general disinterest in the subject, little has been written . . . until now.

The reader of this book is expected to be a software manager or technologist or student who has a basic understanding of what software is, but whose knowledge of maintenance is either rudimentary or has not been updated to include recent developments. It should be particularly useful to the consultant who wants to help computing organizations to a higher quality and more cost-effective maintenance activity; as a component in a university-level course in software engineering; and as on-the-job retraining material for experienced software people.

This book is written with an "equal opportunity" spirit! Neither racial nor sexual stereotypes should be inferred from words like "policeman" or "chairman," and the ubiquitous pronoun "he" should be taken as a third person substitute for the sexless version our language continues to lack.

ACKNOWLEDGEMENT

To the many of you who have contributed to this book, by virtue of an idea, a phrase, an article, or a book, our sincere thanks. The software world will become a better place because each of us strives to improve it.

SOFTWARE MAINTENANCE GUIDEBOOK

One

Introduction

Unfortunately, the nature of hardware and software errors differs in at least one fundamental characteristic—hardware deteriorates because of lack of maintenance, whereas software deteriorates because of the presence of maintenance.*

This is a pop quiz. Quick now, answer these questions without giving them deep thought. Just a simple yes or no will do.

1. Software maintenance consists of correcting the errors in software.
2. Software maintenance is an afterthought kind of thing, and little or no planning is needed for it.
3. Software maintenance consumes only a small slice of the software budget.
4. Software maintenance is a fairly uninteresting subject.

That's it. Just a simple introductory quiz. Now let's do a little self-grading.

---

* "Initial Thoughts on the Pebbleman Process," Institute for Defense Analyses, January 3, 1979; Fisher and Standish.

The correct answer to each of the questions above is "no." Starting with 100, subtract 25 points for each incorrect answer. If your grade is 100, you probably don't need to read much further in this book, except perhaps section 3, where some technology concepts are discussed. If your grade is 75, you are really on top of software as a profession, and deserve congratulations.

But if your grade is 50 or below, do not be chagrined. You are solidly in the majority of the software population. There are a lot of misconceptions and intuitional errors floating around about software maintenance, and you have fallen into them.

The reasons the answers to all of those questions are "no" will all be elaborated in this book. To satisfy your curiosity, though, in brief, those reasons are:

1. Software maintenance involves considerably more change implementation than it does error correction.
2. Traditional software maintenance approaches have pretty much been afterthoughts. However, the result of that inattention is frequently chaotic, unresponsive, and destructive maintenance.
3. Several studies show that software maintenance consumes over half of the software development dollar!
4. With that much money at stake, software maintenance just *has* to be interesting!

The purpose of this pop quiz is to sensitize the reader. Like other areas subject to a lot of stereotypes, software maintenance has been subjected to a veritable cloud of misunderstanding. Most experienced computing professionals and academicians, in spite of their broad knowledge of other aspects of software, are extremely naive about maintenance. It is the purpose of this book to dispel that naivete and those stereotypes, move past them, and provide some techniques and directions for the hopefully newly-interested-in-software-maintenance reader.

(Question 4, whether software maintenance is interesting, was in fact a trick question. Most honest software folk would have answered that it is, indeed, uninteresting. It will be a test of the effectiveness of this book to see if the reader can truthfully change that predicted answer by the time he or she has finished this material!)

Now that you have had the stereotypes exposed, it is time for another pop quiz. Same rules, just a simple yes or no. But keep your guard up!

1. Because of its importance, software maintenance has been the subject of a lot of research studies.
2. Tools and techniques for the maintainer are well known.
3. Software maintenance people are usually the best the computing installation can afford.
4. Management places a lot of emphasis on software maintenance concerns.

Bet you were a little more wary this time! Question 3 was probably a giveaway. Once again the correct answer to each of those questions is "no." The fact of the matter, in a figurative nutshell, is that software maintenance has been a ho-hum subject to just about everybody. Researchers haven't bothered with it; tools and techniques tend to be leftovers from the software developer's toolbox; maintenance assignments are generally thought of as the pits and avoided by all but those who can't pull it off, like the junior folk and the lowest-rated ones; and management, in general, appears to be satisfied with that picture. (Some companies even have to give bonuses to induce people to do maintenance work!)

Like the previous one, this pop quiz had a purpose. If the first was designed to remove the stereotypes, this one was designed to show the aftereffects of those stereotypes. The fact of the matter is that software maintenance has been the subject of colossal blind neglect. Because its significance has been poorly understood, no one has cared to do much about it. The result is an understudied, extremely important technical field.

In that environment, it is difficult to write an effective and useful book. First, there is the problem of motivating readers into moving past the cover. As we have seen, "software maintenance" is a historic turnoff. To make matters worse, there is not a solid body of literature—the work of past maintenance experts—to base a book on.

The only reasonable answer to that dilemma, at least at present, is to create a pioneering book and make it interesting enough to attract

readers who are otherwise turned away by the topic. As mentioned
before, you readers get to issue the grades on *that* pop quiz.

The authors of this book have spent a lot of time maintaining
software. They are also students of computer science, from both an
experiential and an academic point of view. This book is an attempt to
transfer that experience in a meaningful way; to provide a basic
reference point from which the desperately needed future research into
software maintenance can proceed; to give the practicing software
professional and his or her manager the essential information needed
to perform a vital function more effectively; and to provide the student
of software engineering with both perspective and tools to fully
understand the whole spectrum of software activity. Even including
that historically uninteresting field, software maintenance!

1.1   MAINTENANCE IN THE LIFE CYCLE

At a recent computing conference, discussion of the so-called
computing life cycle became a standing joke. Every presenter of every
paper showed a viewfoil or a slide containing his or her graphic version
of the concept. Toward the end of the day, one wag referred to his as
the "obligatory software-life-cycle chart"!

The field of software engineering is by no means immune from fads.
A subject catches the eye of the researcher, and 90% of researchers end
up pouring some energy into that subject. A buzz word comes along
with a new or interesting connotation, and the field is alive with that
buzz word. A concept emerges that promises lowered production costs
and better schedule performance in the delivery of software, and
everyone leaps aboard the bandwagon.

Fortunately, most of these fads have value. Perhaps not as much
value as the number of bandwagon jumpers would indicate, but still
value. The software life cycle is just such a concept, with just such a
value.

The major thrust of this concept is to dispel the myth that the
process of software development is principally the act of coding
software. Some early studies [1] in the late 1960s and early 1970s began
to cast doubts upon that myth and to focus attention on what really did
constitute the software development process. Further study showed
that the analysis of software requirements and the design of the

software consumed far more time than its coding. Just as important, further studies also showed that the checkout and testing of the coded software consumed an even more surprisingly large amount of time. The emergence of the software-life-cycle chart was an attempt to reflect these findings and to graphically illustrate the situation that the factual studies were just beginning to expose.

Many early software-life-cycle charts left out entirely the subject of software maintenance. Just as the early focus had been mistakenly placed on the coding process, the newer focus was still mistakenly placed on the development process. It was not until the mid-1970s that software-life-cycle charts began including software maintenance—and what a profound awakening those pieces of graphic art produced!

It is time for a definition. The *software life cycle* will be defined here as the entire process, from beginning to end, of the development and use of software. That process includes the distinct phases called requirements definition, design, coding, checkout and testing, and maintenance. The reason for calling it a life cycle is probably clear from its definition—it is a womb-to-tomb type of definition, one that pays attention to all of the activities in the software process.

The reason this concept emerged and became popular is only partly dependent on the myths that it exposed and overturned. It is also popular because, in the world where software costs are a major concern, it was becoming obvious that spending money on one software-life-cycle phase could have a profound effect on some of the other phases. For example, putting money (and presumably care) into design would lower the cost of coding, checkout, and testing. Better coding would reduce checkout costs. More effective requirements analysis would lower the cost of every subsequent phase.

This cost-trade argument really became important when the significance of maintenance became clearer. Doing a better job in any of the preceding phases always had a cumulative effect on lowering maintenance costs. Considering how large maintenance costs are, this is of pretty fundamental importance. One whole section of this book, and a lot of comments along the way, will be focused on the task of lowering maintenance costs by spending more careful effort on the up-front life-cycle phases (section 3.2.2.1).

Just as important, the cost trades, prior to life-cycle consideration, had not been obvious. The software producer who delivered software to a customer but had no responsibility to maintain it, for example, might do a slovenly job on some aspects of software development in order to cut costs, with the customer actually incurring higher total cost because of the increased cost of maintaining a slovenly product. With the attention on life-cycle considerations, the customer could direct the developer to do a better job, pay a little more for that better job, and end up with a product whose total cost was less. These economic arguments were fundamental to the popularity of the life-cycle concept.

It is time for a few more definitions. The various phases of the software life cycle are made more specific here.

The first phase in this book will be called *requirements/specifications.* Elsewhere it may be called systems analysis. It is the phase where the problem is being understood and defined. A solution to the problem may evolve during the requirements/specification phase, but it is held in check pending a complete understanding of the problem. Only then should a solution be consciously considered; its representation is then stated in terms of a specification for a software system, and that specification is the primary output of the requirements/specification phase. Perhaps the greatest hazard during this phase is the temptation to define a solution to part of the problem, ignoring the hard parts or those that are ill-defined. Succumbing to this temptation leads to inadequate design and implementation, which in turn leads to revised requirements and major modifications (or, in fact, to "death" of the system). Modification of existing software is probably the greatest plague of the software profession. It is difficult, costly, and frustrating. Many a program has been thrown away and rewritten because it was "unmodifiable." Thus, well-thought-through requirements and specifications are vital to the eventual activities of the software maintainer.

The second phase is the *design* phase. It is time to translate the problem and its requirements specification into a conceptual solution, a blueprint for the actual solution or implementation that will follow. Computing-specific considerations are made: What computer? Which of its resources, and how much? What language? What modules? What sequence of functions? What data structures? What else? All of these ingredients are dumped into the specifications-defined pot, and stirred into a workable and specific plan. The primary output of the design phase is a design representation. It may take the form of words, flowcharts, decision tables, program design language, or any number of other popular or semipopular choices. One of the greatest problems in the design phase is to know when to quit. There is a growing concern that traditional design approaches have been inadequate, quitting too soon, leading to inadequate solutions and a high number of design errors. The opposite concern is equally valid. Grinding a design deeply into the nitty-gritty implementation details wastes time and money since it is at best a replication of the implementation process. A solution to this dilemma—vital to maintenance as well as other aspects of the software life cycle—is still dependent on specific situations.

The third phase is that of *implementation*. The design solution of the previous phase is translated into a computer-readable, computer-processable code. The computer software takes actual shape and becomes an executable, problem-solving entity. The intricacies and vagaries of the computer and the language are met head-on and dealt with. Separate building blocks are constructed and appended to the growing whole. There is the illusion—or perhaps the reality—of crafting a hold-it-in-your-hands product, a Stradivarius capable of making the computer play fine music. The greatest risk is carelessness. Computer programs are a mass of fine details, many of them interrelated and many of them brainbusters in their own right. Ther. is the ever-present danger that carelessness can turn a Stradivarius inᵗ ᴐ a K-Mart toy.

The fourth phase is *checkout*. Checkout is the process of examining and playing the Stradivarius to see if it meets its standards. Checkout is playing Sherlock Holmes to a frustrating series of program-flaw-caused "crimes," sifting through clues to identify (and rehabilitate) the criminals. Checkout is a game played with the program and the computer, where the programmer must both play well and win. Checkout is seeking programming errors, seeking design errors, questioning questionable requirements, and putting the final polish on the soon-to-be-usable computer program. The great hazard here is impatience. Checking out a program must be a painstaking process of trying out all the requirements, all the structural elements, and as many of the combinations of logic paths as common sense and cost/schedule considerations permit. The temptation is to stop short, declare the program fit, and ship it off to its users. The dimensions of this error are monumental. A disgruntled user or maintainer, one who mistrusts a computer program, may never regain that trust. And a computer program can die from lack of trust.

The fifth phase is *maintenance*. Poor old, much disliked maintenance. Maintenance is the process of being responsive to user needs—fixing errors, making user-specified modifications, honing the program to be more useful. Programmers, as we have said, tend to avoid maintenance activities which are usually thought of as lacking the need for creativity. It is ironic that the maintenance programmer, who may be the most important customer relations factor in the software life cycle, is often the least senior, least capable person on the staff. Which brings us to the greatest hazard of maintenance—ineptitude. A finely tuned Stradivarius can be reduced to high-quality fireplace wood by a ham-handed maintainer. All the good of all the previous phases can be undone in the glamorless, unheralded world of maintenance.

Figures 1.1-1 through 1.1-4 graphically illustrate some cost, error, and reliability aspects of the life cycle. They show maintenance as the dominant phase on a cost analysis basis, design as the dominant phase on an error creation basis, and acceptance test and maintenance as

Figure 1.1-1   Software Life Cycle: Costs per Phase

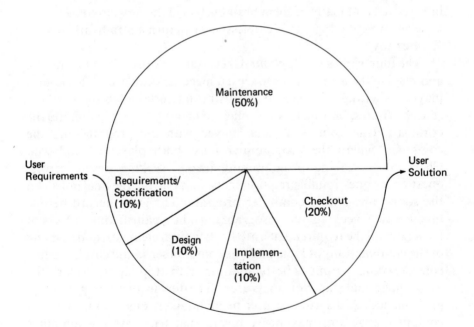

dominant phases on an error discovery basis. These figures are especially interesting in that they display the decidedly nonintuitive data that we have discussed earlier.

Several studies have been conducted on actual costs of the various phases of the software life cycle. Although there are variances between them, figure 1.1-1 presents a roughly accurate breakdown. Note the dominance of the maintenance phase.

REFERENCES

"The High Cost of Software," *Practical Strategies for Developing Large Software Systems,* Addison-Wesley, 1975; Boehm.

"The Economics of Software Quality Assurance," Proceedings of the National Computer Conference, 1976; Alberts.

"Characteristics of Applications Software Maintenance," UCLA Graduate School of Management, 1976; Lientz, Swanson, and Tompkins.

Figure 1.1-2   Software Life Cycle: Error Sources per Phase

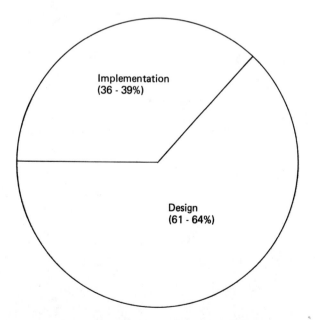

Studies have also been conducted on when during the software-life-cycle errors are generated. These studies typically start after the requirements/specification phase, assuming that the specification is a baseline against which errors are measured. They also typically measure only errors detected after integration or acceptance or delivery. Design errors dominate the picture (Figure 1.1–2).

REFERENCES

"Software Design and Structuring," *Practical Strategies for Developing Large Software Systems,* Addison-Wesley, 1975; Boehm.

"Reliability Measurement during Software Development," Proceedings of the AIAA Conference on Computers in Aerospace, 1977; Hecht, Sturm, and Trattner.

Figure 1.1-3   Software Life Cycle: Error Discovery per Phase

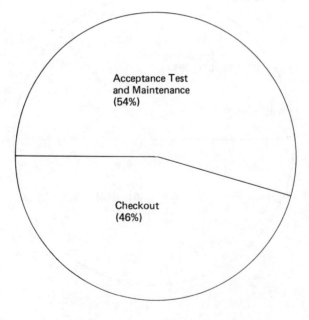

Studies show that errors typically are not detected until very late in the software life cycle, predominantly during or after the acceptance test (Figure 1.1–3).

REFERENCES

"Software Design and Structuring," *Practical Strategies for Developing Large Software Systems,* Addison-Wesley, 1975; Boehm.

Figure 1.1-4   Software Life Cycle: Per Error Fix Cost per Phase

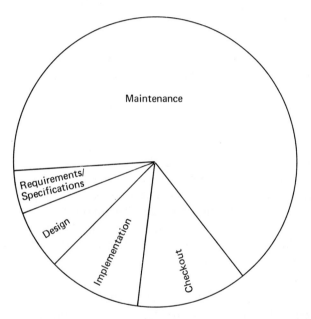

The cost of fixing an error rises dramatically as the software progresses through the life cycle. Maintenance costs (per error) are enormous (Figure 1.1–4).

REFERENCES

Software Acquisition Management Guidebook, Software Maintenance Volume, System Development Corp., TM-5772/004/02, November, 1977; Stanfield and Skrukrud.

1.2 THE MAINTENANCE MINICYCLE

Up until now, this book has avoided making a thorough definition of software maintenance. Since that is the topic of this book, that may strike you as a form of perverse neglect! However, there is a method in this madness.

We have already seen that software maintenance is not what we tend to have thought it was. We would like to think of the software maintainer as the doctor or the auto mechanic whose job is to fix the things that go wrong with the product he knows best. To a limited extent, that is true. But recent studies have shown that the tasks of the software maintenance person are much more complex.

The fact of the matter is that the software maintainer does several things—corrects errors, introduces user-requested changes, adapts the product to new environments, and, in general, makes the software better.

Now we are ready for a definition. *Software maintenance,* for the purposes of this book, is the act of taking a software product that has already been delivered to a customer and is in use by him, and keeping it functioning in a satisfactory way. The word "satisfactory" is deliberately vague, to allow for the inclusion of those facets of software maintenance that we have already hinted at.

In fact, software maintenance can be looked at as the entire range of software development in microcosm. The software maintainer doesn't just throw a wrench on a piece of faulty software, and tighten it, nor does he replace an existing but worn software washer with a new one. Used software is as bright and shiny (or as dull and lusterless!) as the day it was new. The software maintainer isn't a coveralls-clad fixer of spent code; he or she is, instead, a creative implementer of change.

In the process of implementing change, the software maintainer must study the requirements that spawned the change; design a solution to those requirements constrained by the structure of the software to be changed; code that change into the existing software; test the newly changed code; and—deja vu!—become responsible for maintaining the revised software system.

If all that sounds familiar, it should. We have just reiterated the words of the previous section. The software maintainer is *not* just a software maintainer—he or she is also a systems analyst, a designer, a coder, and a tester.

12

In that sense, the word "maintenance" is a misnomer. The software maintainer has a creative, if frustrating, role to play in the software life cycle. In many ways, it is a more versatile role than that of the analyst who doesn't code or the coder who doesn't test.

1.3   PERFECTIVE, ADAPTIVE, CORRECTIVE MAINTENANCE

There is another way in which the word "maintenance" is a misnomer. We have already mentioned that software is not just the fixing of errors; in fact, changing software due to revised requirements is far more frequent than is changing software due to problems or errors. Not only is this the case, but statistically and experientially it has been shown that the error-fixing part of software maintenance is far down the pushdown stack of maintenance activities.

In an important study [2], it was shown that maintenance activities actually break into three main subactivities. Those subactivities, and the ways in which a maintainer's time is spread among them, are discussed below.

1.3.1   Perfective Maintenance

Perfective maintenance is the act of improving the software's function by responding to customer- and programmer-defined changes. This is *not* the portion of software maintenance that is involved with fixing errors. But it *is* the biggest maintenance time consumer. According to ref. [2], 60% of the software maintainer's time is spent on these "make better" changes.

1.3.2   Adaptive Maintenance

Software does not exist in a vacuum. Instead, it is part of a total system environment, and its relationship to that environment is critical to its ability to do its part of the total system job. *Adaptive maintenance* is the act of changing software to adapt to environmental changes. If the computer on which the software runs is going to use a new operating system, or the total system data base must have some detail level changes (for example, if the ZIP code is increased from five to nine characters), the software must be adapted to those changes. According to ref. [2], 18% of software maintenance is adaptive.

1.3.3   Corrective Maintenance

Now we finally get to the data item you've been looking for! The pure correction of software errors, dubbed *corrective maintenance,* consumes only 17% of the maintainer's time [2]. Thus, maintenance of software is indeed unlike traditional maintenance activities. (The alert reader may have noticed that the various percentages given above do not sum to 100. Reference [2] allocates the remaining 5% to "other.")

1.4   DEFINITIONS

Hopefully, the overall concepts of software maintenance have now been grasped. It has been shown that this kind of maintenance is nontraditional, since it encompasses all phases of the life cycle and is much more perfective than it is corrective.

Before we move into further chapters, where more detailed aspects of software maintenance are dealt with, it is time to pause one last time and look around at some generic concepts. To that end, the following definitions are offered:

Maintenance was defined in section 1.2. For the sake of provoking thought, however, an alternative definition is presented here. Maintenance is the phase of the software life cycle to which development costs are sometimes transferred. This is a tongue-in-cheek definition, included to highlight the fact that whatever the developer doesn't do will probably end up being done as maintenance.

A *customer* is the person who wants to use the software. The customer may or may not actually pay for the software—again, the meaning is somewhat nontraditional—but he or she will become the software *user* when the software is *delivered.*

The *system* is the total problem solution. The system is usually considerably larger than one or two programs and/or subroutines, and may, in fact, include nonsoftware components such as computer hardware and documentation. The emphasis of this book, it should be mentioned, is on system-sized solutions, not program-sized solutions.

This book does not address itself to the maintenance of 100-line programs. In general, the maintenance of a program of this size is no more taxing than the effort that went into its design and development. The real area of need, and the area tackled by this book, is maintenance of the several-man-year software solution.

Complexity is the measure of difficulty in understanding and maintaining a piece of software. Complexity is to be minimized to the extent possible by both the developer and the maintainer. This means constant attention to such things as the size of a software system's component modules, the logic structure of those modules, and the interactions between modules. Modules whose complexity is excessive are those that cannot be grasped in one "brain-length." It is an irony of software life that complex software can frequently not even be understood by its creator, let alone its maintainer.

The overview of software maintenance activities shown in figure 1.4-1 (see page 16) is meant to set the stage for the more detailed discussion that follows. Note that the requirements, design, and implementation lead to the creation of the system. Note further that interacting with the system are both the customer and the maintainer, each with his or her own documentation (the user manual and the maintenance manual, respectively). The customer poses questions and problems to the maintainer, and the answers to those questions are, where appropriate, filtered through a change control process and back into the system. Each of those concepts, and more, will be explored further in the material that follows.

1.5   REFERENCES

1.   "The High Cost of Software," *Practical Strategies for Developing Large Software Systems,* Addison-Wesley, 1975; Boehm.

   Discusses the cost of software, and how that cost is broken down over the software-life-cycle phases. Sees coding as the least-cost item (compared to requirements definition, design and testing).

2.   "Characteristics of Application Software Maintenance," Communications of the ACM, June 1978; Lientz, Swanson and Tompkins.

   Surveys 69 computing installations to identify the characteristics of software maintenance. Describes what maintenance is like in a typical data-processing computing shop.

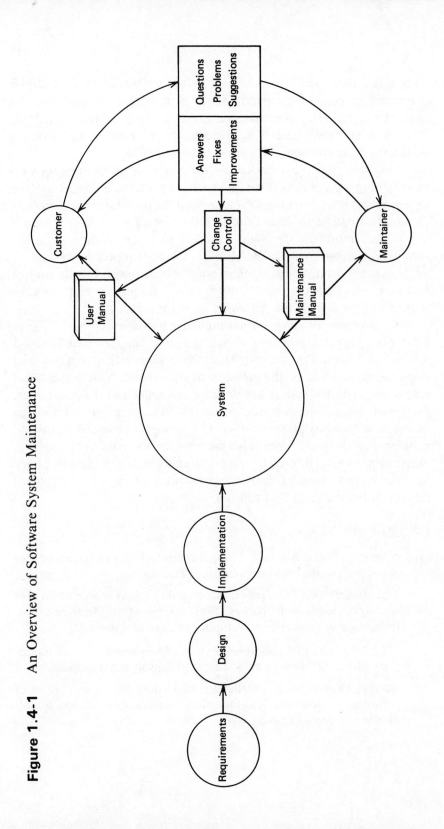

Figure 1.4-1 An Overview of Software System Maintenance

Two

The People Side of Maintenance

The role of the individual in the process of software development is a fascinating one, the peripheral subject of a lot of otherwise-focused studies into software productivity. Current opinions range from one extreme—deemphasizing the individual in favor of the team (described unsympathetically in ref. [16], even to the point of striving for "egoless programming" [32]—to another—the quality of the individual is seen as the greatest single factor impacting software product quality [10, 20, 23, 27, 29]. Some recent studies take positions in between [5, 36].

In some ways, these varying opinions are irrelevant to the current social milieu in which software development finds itself. Because of the dramatic and constantly increasing impact of computers on our lives, there has been a shortage of skilled software developers almost from the beginning of computing as a field. Current projections show the situation getting worse (or better, depending on whether you're a software-skilled person or not!) for at least the next five years. Some computing installations are currently functioning at only 75% of the software skills they require. For all the debate about how much individual quality can be used vis-à-vis team-oriented quantity, the fact of the matter is that there is not enough individual quality to go around. Many software problems simply *must* be solved by mediocre people instead of top-quality people. Software planners and manners must take that fact into account.

Over the years, many attempts have been made to lower the skill level required of software people. In the early 1960s, some predictions were made that with the proper tools, "grocery clerks" could be trained to be programmers. The "proper tools" of that era were the COBOL language and automated software writing tools. In retrospect, that opinion is almost laughable. Yet researchers continue to tout, and managers continue to fund, modern-day equivalents of the grocery clerk philosophy. The goal of converting from software as a cottage industry to software as an assembly line process continues to be sought after . . . and to be elusive.

In the mid-1960s one leading computer hardware firm, believing that it had produced the proper set of tools to permit semiautomated production of system software, bet a product line on using unskilled programmers to build compilers, assemblers, and link loaders. The bet lost—the resulting products were grotesquely inefficient—and not only the software but the hardware product line was a failure in the marketplace [11].

Here we have, then, the seeds of a dilemma: too few people to do too many increasingly complex software jobs, and no escape methodology identified. The dilemma becomes visible in the increasing number of square inches of "Programmers Wanted" advertisements in the trade journals, and the escalating salaries of programmers, especially new hirees. (In fact, a more subtle and more complicated dilemma emerges as demand and inflation skip merrily along hand in hand—the new hiree often gets more money than the one- or two-year "veteran" programmer.)

The dilemma is especially relevant to software maintenance. It is especially relevant because, for all the debate about team versus individual contributions, and quality versus quantity performance, *software maintenance remains a bastion of the individual worker.* For better or worse, software maintainers are most often individual contributors, soloing untended among the lines of code of one or more programs for which they alone have responsibility. This is not universally true—team maintenance is also used. But maintenance has grown up like the weed patch in the garden of software production. As a result, maintenance is the arena of the ad hoc gardener. If he is a good gardener, then this ignoring of the field is not harmful. But if he is a bad gardener, the weed patch may well consume the garden.

All of this is a prelude to the unique people problems of the field of software maintenance. Ad hoc it is. Individualistic it often is. Disdained, it certainly is. Yet here is where over 50% of the software dollar is spent! The people side of software maintenance obviously deserves some special focus.

There are many names used to describe software maintainers—some derogatory, some flattering. Perhaps one of the best is "unsung heroes." The song of these unsung heroes will take form in the following sections of this book—what talents a maintainer needs, what techniques are or should be at his disposal, what his problems are likely to be, how those problems should be prioritized, when the individualist and when the team roles are appropriate, and so on—in short, the maintainer as a person is dealt with.

2.1   PUTTING THE PEOPLE PROBLEM IN PERSPECTIVE

Perhaps the importance of the skill level needed for software maintenance can best be put in perspective by the following*:

> There is a problem of very deep and insidious consequences for the activity of maintenance. Some errors in software consist not of trivial diagnosable and treatable faults at the programming level, but rather of subtle "logic" errors in the design or implementation.
>
> The problem is that a "logic" error may occur at any of a number of levels of program representation spanning the gap from the problem domain to the concrete implementation domain.
>
> To make this situation vivid, consider a navigation module on a supersonic aircraft. Let us suppose that the navigation module is supposed to provide the correct position of the aircraft to within 10 meters anywhere in the atmosphere of the earth. The module obtains input from gyros, accelerometers, clocks, doppler radars, and navigation signal receptors which can listen to satellite and ground station signals. Suppose it has been determined (perhaps by exercise of self-diagnosing interface monitoring procedures and execution of fault-

---

*From "Initial Thoughts on the Pebbleman Process," an analysis of the requirements for the environment for the Department of Defense Ada programming language, and written by David A. Fisher (Institute for Defense Analyses) and Thomas A. Standish (University of California, Irvine).

detection decision trees) that none of the input devices is malfunctioning. But suppose that the results produced by the module are consistently in error.

Let us further suppose that the actual error is a superimposition of errors from three separate sources: (1) a simple programming error involving unintentional clobbering of the contents of a global variable by a local procedure which incorrectly assumes that the global variable is local, (2) the decay in numerical accuracy of a certain class of computations through inadequate numerical analysis of error propagation, and (3) failure to design the module to take account of coriolis force, leading to systematic errors on north-south trajectories at high mach numbers.

Each of these three error sources might fall within the province of distinct skills at the command of distinct trained specialists. Only a physicist familiar with the laws of kinematics and dynamics might be expected to realize and correct the coriolis force error. Only a numerical analyst familiar with the laws of numerical error propagation might be expected to discover and correct the error of numerical accuracy decay. And only a programmer trained in the use of nomenclature scope rules in the programming language used to implement the module might be expected to discover and correct the error of unintentional information clobbering.

If the actual error is a superimposition of these three sorts of errors at these three sorts of levels of program logic, it is doubtful that a maintainer, trained only in one of the three relevant skills, could succeed in untangling the superimposed errors, in isolating their sources, and in making appropriate corrections.

In a similar vein, if the system is being enhanced to meet new requirements, the skills of requirement analysts and designers may be required to modify the requirements and the design incrementally and to bring the requirements and design documents up-to-date consistent with the enhancement. In fact, because of the presence of more constraints, incremental reanalysis and redesign might be more difficult than original analysis and design. It may not be enough for the maintainer skilled only in the implementation, test, and integration phases of the software life cycle to perform acts of enhancement that call for the replay of skills exercised by teams of skilled specialists at earlier life cycle phases—teams now disbanded and unavailable. This is particularly likely to be true if the requirements and design levels of the system being enhanced demand skilled thinking in application domains widely separate from programming.

But we know that maintenance and enhancement may tend to occur under circumstances under which the original teams that performed the high level logic analysis and design (and which used special application domain skills remote from programming skills) have long since disbanded, leaving maintenance and enhancement tasks to those unskilled in the higher logic levels of the system. Such maintenance circumstances are unpropitious unless techniques can be found to determine when to call in or recongregate teams of skilled specialists needed for fault detection, repair, or enhancement.

Some of these problems of maintenance are thus deep, vexing, and expensive.

One of the reviewers of this book* put another perspective on the same subject, the skill level needed for software maintenance:

1. Maintenance is intellectually very difficult (complex). Problems cannot be bounded—the cause could be anywhere.
2. Maintenance is technically very difficult. Problems cannot be specialized—they could be in the coding, design, architecture, or concept.
3. Maintenance is unfair. Information required is not available, or is wrong. The problem-causing person got promoted or took a better job and didn't finish the write-up. Even finished write-ups don't help most of the time because programmers don't know what to put in them.
4. Maintenance is no-win. People only come to maintenance with problems.
5. Maintenance work is dirty. Good maintenance is done behind the scenes, with the code and the machines. There is very little glory, noticeable progress, or chance for "success."
6. Maintenance lives in the past. The general quality of code being maintained is often terrible—partly because it's old, created when everybody's understanding of software was more rudimentary; and because a lot of code is produced by people before they become really good!

For all of these reasons, maintenance is hardly the place to assign your new hirees or lowest-rated programmers!

2.2   PERSONALITY PROFILE OF THE MAINTAINER

There is a danger in the "unsung hero" image of the software maintainer—the danger of taking the image too seriously! Certainly, it would be possible to draw up a set of requirements for the software supermaintainer that would call for a person who could leap several tall buildings in an optimum number of bounds while keeping pace

*Robert J. Rader of The Software Developers.

with a speeding locomotive. Such glowing fantasy would be counter-productive to the goal of a realistic understanding of what is expected of the software maintainer, and a source of embarrassment to the unsung hero himself.

Yet the realities of the software maintenance world are a miniature of that fantasy. Remember that software maintenance is a microcosm of the entire software development process. There is the maintainer—doing a systems analysis of a problem area leading to a requirements definition; changing gears to designer and outlining the impact of the requirements on the product; coding his or her own design solution; testing and verifying the results; and releasing the revised product to the user world. In an era of increasing specialization, where often analysts analyze and designers design and coders code and testers test, the maintainer must do all of these things—and do them well.

And more. The maintainer also plays a customer liaison role, holding the customer's hand on anomalous outputs, negotiating with the customer on the shape of change results, interpreting the computer's oblique job control language needs, and, in general, serving as the front line of the image that the computing installation has for its customers. Perhaps the Unsung Hero who dons the supermaintainer cape can be forgiven his occasional excesses!

At the risk of increasing the danger of taking this image too seriously, a profile of personality characteristics that a maintainer should have is presented below. The point of this profile is to emphasize the diverse and unique requirements placed on the maintainer. They are requirements for traits that many programmers do not possess.

2.2.1   Flexibility

The software maintainer must be able to adapt to styles of code that are not his (or her) own. He must be able to distinguish between code that is "bad" (e.g., poorly modularized or poorly structured) and code that he doesn't like (perfectly good code but done differently from the way he would have done it). The importance of the ability to make this judgment, and of being flexible, is that the maintainer must *not* spend time redoing code simply because he doesn't like it; yet he must, in order to achieve the goal of making the program more maintainable (over a period of time), gradually replace the "bad" code. To an extent not yet well defined in the literature, programmers have individualized styles of coding. The flexible maintainer is able to live with and accept a variety of such styles. (The subject of style is dealt with more fully in section 2.3.)

2.2.2   Broad Background

In order to be flexible, the programmer must have been exposed to a variety of programming styles. The originating programmer will have imposed his background on the code. For example, a heavily Fortran-oriented programmer will write his program in a Fortran-like manner, even if he is coding in COBOL. The maintainer of a system should be well versed in many different languages to be able to recognize the subtleties of various styles of code when he encounters them.

In addition, the maintainer should be well versed in a variety of relevant application disciplines. A programmer rarely will spend a whole career dealing with only one kind of customer. The report for the company comptroller, for example, may have a different set of emphases than the report for the chief engineer.

2.2.3   Patience

The maintainer's life holds two areas where patience will aid him. The first of these is in liaison with the customer. Obviously, the customer has a job to do, and he is using the system to assist him. He probably knows very well what he wants it to do—but the maintainer usually knows better what it will really do, and why. The maintainer will encounter some very impatient users who will want to know why the program doesn't do what they expect it to do. The seeds are sown for a monumental clash if the maintainer is not capable of bridging this knowledge gap between expectations and capabilities.

The second place where patience will pay for the maintainer is in the area of product stability. The customer will usually demand stability of the system. He will not tolerate sudden drastic differences in the method of operation of his product. As a result of this, the introduction of a radical new program piece may either be prohibited, or at least phase-delayed, even if the maintainer knows that it will eventually be a major improvement to the system. Take, for example, a piece of code that is extremely complicated and "almost" correct, but a real bear to maintain. The maintainer's options boil down to (1) redesigning the entire process, using different techniques and unraveling and removing all the bugs, or (2) evolving the program into something better. The demand for stability may make the evolutionary process the proper choice. As each problem impacting the messy code is reported, a quick and dirty fix is installed to correct the erroneous processing, but along with this a long-term approach is taken with an eye toward gradually untangling the mess. At each release of the system, small improvements are incorporated. After a long time, the program begins to approach a reasonably easy to modify state. Obviously, the impatient maintainer will find it difficult to compromise "goodness" in favor of the evolutionary requirements of stability.

2.2.4   Self-motivation

The maintainer, it has already been pointed out, often works as an individual, with little team or management intervention. For the maintainer's time to be productive, he must be able to self-start and self-proceed. The maintainer who needs constant management prodding probably should not be a maintainer. The maintainer who can create his own excitement will have gone a long way toward creating self-motivation.

2.2.5   Responsibility

The twin to self-motivation is responsibility. The maintainer must feel some sort of pride of workmanship and pride of product. Given that, he will then take responsibility for the quality and quantity of his work. Without that sense of responsibility, the independently working maintainer can waste enormous quantities of time before he is found out. Worse yet, he may wreak havoc in a previously well defined piece of code. A sense of responsibility probably underlies all the other personality traits that a maintainer must have.

2.2.6   Humility

This "perfect person" who may have more than he reasonably expects to do in a lifetime will be hit on one or more occasions with angry customers proclaiming "Your program screwed up." Now's the time for an egoless programmer! He must be able to withstand the harshest forms of criticism and not allow it to destroy his effectiveness. The humble programmer, to be a good maintenance programmer, must be able to have his nose shoved in his mistakes and come up smiling. "I screwed up again, didn't I?"—even said through clenched teeth—can go a long way toward disarming an angry customer and making him into a willing and able proponent of a still-faulty program. A sense of humor is definitely an asset to the humble programmer [7].

2.2.7 Innovation

Here's a real tough one for the software maintainer. You give him an already existing program product, with all the bells and whistles and warts and wrinkles that implies; and you ask him to flexibly and flawlessly adapt to its style and content. Then along comes a major change request—one that proposes to add a fundamentally new capability to the product, let's say. One for which the product was not originally designed, let's even say.

The requirement is now "innovate." Bend this somewhat unwilling product into a wholly new form. But with minimal impact on the existing structure!

Surely this is the most taxing kind of innovation—the kind that says: "Within the constraints of what is, please create something new." The requirement for constrained innovation is certainly the hardest to ask of a software maintainer—but for a large and complex software product, thousands or hundreds of thousands of dollars may ride on the ability to innovate.

2.2.8 Historian

The software maintainer needs to keep track of what has gone on, with some evaluation of why. An appropriate chronology of the system must be maintained. There are various places where this may be performed. A chronological list of error reports as filed will maintain some semblance of historical perspective. Annotating changes to the system chronologically, or by version, or by problem report number is a vital piece of product history. Producing version release notices with notations concerning problems reported and any significant events will also aid in the history. The software maintainer must often be able to look back on what he has done in order to look forward to where he is going. (See section 3.2.3.1 for a more complete discussion of the historian's job.)

2.3   STYLES AND STYLE CLASHES

A great deal of research is currently being done into ways of making programming better and programmers more capable, software less complex, and solving other similar vital software concerns. Most of this research is oriented toward solving the pressing problems of high software cost and slipped software schedules and low software reliability. As management concerns, these are the Big Picture crux of the state of the software art.

But down at the technical level, where the development programmer and the maintenance programmer spend their days fabricating the software products out of some language's syntax and semantics, there is a different set of concerns. These concerns are centered on an intangible entity that some software people refer to as "style." And for the most part, there is little research focused in this area.

That is not, of course, entirely true. A significant number of papers in the 1960s and early 1970s extolled the virtues of modular programming (e.g., [21, 25]). A veritable avalanche of papers in the 1970s spread the gospel of structured programming (e.g., [1, 4]). A few specific works have discussed the generic concept of style [14, 17, 31, 36]. A recent Association for Computing Machinery Turing lecture dealt with the importance of style (as well as generic algorithms), calling the underlying concepts "paradigms" [9].

In addition, an enormous amount of research effort is poured into the design and occasional implementation of new programming languages. (Some of the best, in recent years, are Pascal [33, 34], Modula [35], and Euclid [28].)

But "style," although touched on by all of these efforts, is something more than all of them. Style is, perhaps, best described as the result of blending a problem to be solved, a programmer providing a solution, and one or more solution methodologies. The resulting program has a style that has been impacted by all elements of the blend. Only in the context of a program is it really possible to discuss style.

All of the above is still, however, an evasion of what is needed here—a working definition of the term "style." Meeting the problem head-on but not forgetting the inexactness of the concept, which makes definition difficult—we make this definition: *Style is the imprint placed on a computer program by the programmer and the methodologies he uses.*

The relevance of the subject of style to software maintenance is, as has been alluded to previously, important. A given program contains an imprinted style. A given programmer possesses a certain backgrou ı that orients him toward certain styles. If a programmer is assigned ₀o maintain a program whose style is too different from his own, a style clash results. The programmer's reaction, if he is inflexible, may be to throw out the program rather than adjust to its style. In fact, style clashes are the cause of a great deal of software "reinvention of the wheel," where the same program is written over and over again. It is interesting to speculate on the early efforts of the computing field in the 1950s, and similar efforts in the early days of the microcomputer field in the 1970s, to share software. To a large extent these efforts have failed, and high among a complexity of causes is surely the inability of sharing programmers to solve the style clash problem. (One legacy of the sharing concept is a leading hardware company users' group, still called SHARE, even though the formative concept of users sharing code among themselves has been all but dead in the organization for more than 20 years!)

It is easy nowadays to pooh-pooh the notion of style and the problem of style clashes. For one thing, the doctrine of structured programming is founded on the notion that there is one best way to program, and structured programming advocates would tend to say that mass adherence to this discipline would solve such problems. For another thing, there is a large body of data which says that the actual act of programming is an inconsequential part of overall software development costs, and thus the issue of style is an inconsequential one.

These arguments, at least in the domain of software maintenance, are easily rebutted. Software should possess structured programming. But it by no means encompasses the entire area of style. Structured programming by itself, for instance, is largely mute on the vital area of software modularity: How should modules be selected to make the program easy to develop and maintain? In the opinion of the authors, program modularity contributes far more toward software style than program "structure" does, although both are important.

The unimportance of coding as a part of overall software costs came as a shock to most software technologists. We are in an era where that shock is being absorbed. One impact of the shock has been to try to divert the focus of software concern to its other life-cycle areas, such as requirements definition and design, and testing and verification. But there is one domain in which this shock effect may be too thorough—software maintenance. The importance of code to the software maintainer remains undiminished—it may have cost less to create than we realized, but it is still the stuff that the maintainer modifies and manipulates. And remembering that maintenance is more than 50% of the software effort, some measure of lost perspective is regained—coding, for all its unimportance in the development phases, is still a vital part of the whole software process.

And so is style. And so are style clashes.

This discussion, however, remains elusively philosophical. In the paragraphs that follow, the issue will be brought into better focus. As a first attempt at a taxonomy of styles, the organization of the discussion will use languages as the separating element. This organization is chosen for historic convenience and not out of any conviction that it is a best organization. In fact, the whole issue of style deserves further research and development attention. (The importance of this issue is still only hinted at in the literature [30]. But in some industrial environments, one programmer is chosen to be responsible for imposing a consistent style on a system, rewriting code where necessary.) One of the better discussions of this topic to date, emerging from an attempt to define "traditional programming" in contrast to "structured programming," is found in ref. [2]. The issue of software complexity is inextricably related to style [13].

2.3.1   Assembly Program Style

The best place to start discussing style from a chronological point of view is the worst place to start from a definitive point of view. Assembly programming, the cradle of all software efforts, is also a carte blanche of programming style. This is not to say that assembly programs cannot and do not have style—quite the contrary is true. Rather, assembly language, via its access to all the capabilities a computer possesses, permits an enormous variety in styles.

In assembly code, for example, it is possible to produce a hideously modularized, impossibly structured program which would offend any programmer's notion of acceptable style. But it is also possible to produce an impeccably modularized, reasonably well structured program in assembly code. And, via macro facilities much beloved by many assembly code advocates, it is even possible to produce a *very* well structured assembly program.

Historically, however, assembly code has tended to be a bastion of software characteristics which, although sometimes vital in particular contexts, are generally considered to be stylistically poor:

1. Tricky programs (for the sake of efficiency)
2. Self-modifying programs (to overcome hardware instruction set limitations)
3. Hardware-dependent programs (because they are sometimes necessary and easiest to provide in assembly code)
4. Standards-defying programs (because sometimes problems and standards are incompatible!)

Thus, the assembly program impact on the subject of style can be summarized in one word: "eclectic." The following paragraphs will contribute more toward defining the term by example.

2.3.2 Fortran Program Style

Fortran was the first language to significantly disturb the assembly programmer's sacred communion with computer hardware. And, judging by contemporary usage, it may well also continue until it is the last! Love it or leave it, Fortran is one methodology which has had a significant impact on style.

The best thing that can be said about the style which has emerged naturally among Fortran users is its modularity. Fortran pioneered the concept of modularity into a language form, the SUBROUTINE (although the concept itself originated among assembly programmers). In fact, Fortran's plethora of subroutine and function capabilities constituted almost a mandate to write modular code. The well-defined application library which accompanies most Fortrans is an impressive example of modular programming's advantages.

But communication of data among these modules was solved to a lesser level of satisfaction. Call sequences were an effective communication device, but for large masses of data, the common block, a sometimes error-prone communication media, was invented. Common blocks became an important and difficult area of Fortran style.

Naming of entities in Fortran is even more unsatisfactory. Data names are limited to an unyielding and inadequate six characters. Program structure is likewise limited, and statements are numbered rather than named. The resulting Fortran style leads to programs largely devoid of intrinsic readability.

And at the bottom of the style hierarchy lies Fortran's total inadequacy in data structuring. In spite of the common need to declare non-word-oriented entities in almost all application areas, Fortran provides no such capability at all, and even attempts to resolve the problem with part-word-manipulating library routines which force imperative statement solutions for a problem that should be solved at the declarative level. Thus, Fortran style is a mixed bag—the beauty of well-designed modularity, frayed around the edges by serious lacks. The Fortran programmer tends to write difficult-to-read, declarationally inadequate programs. And because of the pervasity of Fortran, this style is also very pervasive.

2.3.3   COBOL Program Style

In many ways, COBOL style is almost a mirror image of Fortran. Its data-declaration capabilities are extremely impressive—the ability to specify editing of data in a declaration instead of in executable code or the pseudo-executable Fortran format, for instance, is elegant in its power and flexibility.

And COBOL file input/output, tailored to its application area needs, is also well done. COBOL style is good in many areas where it needs to be good.

But modularity, in contrast, is badly lacking. The ability to perform paragraphs simply is no substitute for the parameter-passing, common-communicating Fortran subroutine.

To add to an emerging distastefulness, COBOL forces the programmer into a taxing verbosity of syntax and a straitjacket of keyword and syntactic requirements which lead to programs that are slow to write without very much increased readability.

The availability of certain extremely flexible general-purpose modules, such as sort packages and report generators, helps redeem the COBOL notion of style. Basically, though, the COBOL style is a study in contrasts—the power of excellent data structuring and thorough input/output—and the weakness of awkward syntax and omitted modularity. Predictably, the COBOL programmer's style is a natural clash with that of the Fortran programmer.

2.3.4   Algol Program Style

Algol is a peculiarity in any discussion of style. Although Algol has been little used in production program environments (except in Europe), its impact on style is as significant as that of Fortran and COBOL.

Algol's forte is the structured program. In contrast to COBOL's powerful data-structuring capability, Algol allowed the programmer to specify structure in a series of executable statements which could be treated as one and grouped for readability. It provided far more satisfying conditional constructs than either Fortran or COBOL, and was at least their equal for looping.

And, mending part of the Fortran data-declaration dilemma, Algol provided for hierarchic data declarations, with data being capable of being localized to a particular domain of a program. Further improving on Fortran, Algol also permitted the programmer to create somewhat self-documenting programs by allowing data, program, and statements to have meaningful names.

But alas, Algol had its share of weaknesses also. Its subroutine capability, in some ways stronger than Fortran's in that it allowed subroutines to be declared within other programs and even nested and especially recursive, still failed to provide for separate compilation, an important element of modularity.

And its input/output was simply nonexistent. Both COBOL with its file-oriented I/O, and Fortran with its Formats, at least had some input/output style. But Algol has none to call its own.

Algol, including of course its many successors, thus spawns a third style distinct from both Fortran's and COBOL's. On the whole more satisfying, with structured and fairly modular programs, Algol still tended to create a style in which programs were large (with many internal subprograms) and devoid of any common input/output characteristics.

2.3.5   Other Program Style

As the style deficiencies of the previously mentioned languages have been discovered, computer linguists have pressed for their resolution and correction. Supplementing Fortran's modularity and COBOL's declarative power and Algol's structure are improvements on all three concepts. "Clusters," for example, may be declared which both share and bound access to a common set of functions and a function-dependent data base. Constants, both computational and declarative, may be named to permit safe and easy modification. Language forms that optimize structure and minimize complexity (to the extent possible) are provided.

Clearly, the Fortran style and the COBOL style and the Algol style are all acceptably imperfect. So are the improvements mentioned in the preceding paragraph. The thrust of this discussion on style is *not* to press for a best style to the exclusion of all others. It is, rather, to point out one set of historic reasons why varying styles have evolved, and why style clashes are inevitable.

The maintenance programmer does himself and his institution a favor when he acknowledges the validity of acceptably imperfect programming styles, strives to correct those which are unacceptably imperfect, and, in general, lives comfortably within the constraints of the methodologies available to him. The maintenance programmer who cannot do this may well destroy more code in his lifetime than he produces.

The style clash, then, is a study in subjective judgments. In general, the programmer should be encouraged to flexibly overcome such clashes. But there *are* occasions where tolerance overdone can be an affront to common sense. With large dollars riding on the outcome of such judgments, the style clash and its ramifications deserve more than the passing attention that they have gotten in the literature and by management.

2.4 GOALS AND PRIORITIES

It will come as no surprise to the alert reader that the goals of software maintenance are not as straightforward as might be superficially imagined. The obvious goal of fixing errors is simply one among many. In fact, because of the complexity of software maintenance goals, it is worth naming them and discussing their relative priorities. Keeping not only the goals but the priorities in mind can save the software maintainer from potentially tragic blunders. It will be seen that the software maintenance person, already charged with many important technical tasks, must also be responsible for juggling a set of administrative goals and priorities.

2.4.1 Software Reliability

In the context of this book, reliability is the ability of the customer to use the software and get correct results. This is always the top-priority goal of the software maintainer. No amount of maintenance heroics can take the place of software reliability.

If a software product becomes unstable due to frequent changes, get it working again and then don't touch it for awhile. Stockpile your subsequent changes, or sit on your thumbs, if necessary—but don't tinker with the product until its credibility has been restored.

2.4.2 Error Correction

If a software error is discovered, it is usually—but not always—important to fix it as soon as possible. In general, error correction is the second-highest-priority goal of the software maintainer.

There are, however, exceptions. Maintaining software reliability is one—it may be better to let an error go for a while if the alternative is to risk blowing up a customer's upcoming run. The nature of the error is another. Errors come in many flavors, from those which totally inhibit use of the program to those which are so unusual that they may be encountered once in a millennium, with all the waystops in between. The priority of correcting an error must be directly related to the seriousness of the error itself. And in some extreme cases, the cost of fixing an error may be more than the value of the fix, in which case the error should never be corrected!

2.4.3 Change Requests

Analogous to correcting errors is the goal of making changes. Assuming that the change has been sanctified by some authorizing agent (see section 4.2.1), making that change is a fairly high priority goal. However, as with errors, specific changes come in various priority flavors.

In general, fixes should be given higher priority than changes. But clearly a high-priority change could be done before a low-priority fix. The establishment of relative priorities for fix and change specific cases should be negotiated and clearly agreed upon between the maintainer and his customer.

2.4.4 Software Maintainability

Perhaps the most surprising goal of software maintenance is maintenance for the sake of maintenance. It is sometimes a little hard to explain to a manager that a specific modification is not tied to any specific problem report or change request [12]. But untangling a messy program, or generalizing a special-purpose one, or annotating an unreadable one may in the long run be a more important maintenance activity than fixing errors. To the extent that the program becomes easier to maintain, its useful life is extended. Still, in most cases this goal must be kept in perspective. In the scheduling of maintenance activities, it should almost always have lower priority than those already mentioned.

2.4.5 Software Efficiency

Software consumes lots of resources—storage space, computer time, people energy, and more. Efficiency is here treated generically as the optimization of one or more of those resources. Obviously, making a program more efficient is another valid software maintenance goal.

Again, this kind of goal must be measured against the importance of the resource problem. If a program won't fit in memory, or runs longer than the hardware's MTBF, then the priority of enabling that efficiency is extremely high! But generally, efficiency considerations rank at or near the bottom of the priority ladder.

2.4.6 Documentation

The intelligent software maintainer should realize, almost intuitively, that keeping documentation up to date is a vital part of any software change activity. It is a task analogous to the craftsman in another field keeping his toolbox organized and his tools oiled.

Unfortunately, this intuition is all too frequently lacking. Therefore, in the spirit of saying an "it goes without saying," the priority of the documentation of the impact of a change is such that it should be completed immediately after the change is completed and before another is begun.

This subsection, it should be pointed out, does not appear in priority sequence as did the others in this section. Documentation is *not* the lowest-priority software change activity; instead, its priority is essentially that of the task it is associated with, and its activity should be completed coincident with that task.

Note that the impact of this activity is considerably lessened using the philosophy of this book—that detail documentation be contained in the listing (this is discussed further in section 4.3). Presumably, the maintenance programmer incorporated his commentary when he wrote his revised code (if not, it can be added in one last pass over the code). For many changes, the impact will be below the level of the formal documentation, and thus *it* need not be changed at all. The task of document updating may, in many cases, be relatively trivial.

2.5 CONSTRAINTS ON MODIFICATIONS

A president of the United States, in a televised address to the people, once said that adapting social security payments to the cost of living was a hard problem because "it's computerized, and those computers are awfully hard to change." What he meant, of course, was that the software that controls social security processing was hard to change. Computer people, used to taking the blame for a lot of human data manipulation types of problems, tended to pooh-pooh the comment as one born of ignorance. Headline treatment of so-called "computer foul-ups" has become commonplace. So has the fact that deeper investigation shows that the computer itself, and its software, have seldom been the problem. But one leading computer professional, discussing the incident, said that the president "may have been right. Simple-sounding changes can often be maddeningly difficult to effect. Designing for flexibility is costly and difficult; we need much better systems analysis and programming tools."*

Earlier in this book, we mentioned the problem of innovation within constraints. It is important to spend a little more time on that issue. For better or for worse, an existing piece of software has both a style and a structure. If, as suggested above, it was designed with particular care, it may even have a somewhat flexible style and (to the extent that it makes sense!) a flexible structure. But flexibility can only go so far. Flexibility stems from the designer's ability to anticipate the kinds of changes that the software may need over its life span. No matter how potent the crystal ball, there are severe limitations on any human being's ability to see very far ahead. Particularly in a century where human beings have learned to fly, send words and pictures invisibly through the air, and to make devices that appear to think and reason, it would be astounding if a software designer were able to anticipate all the uses or abuses his newly conceived software might be put to.

One major controversy in the data processing (DP) field as the 1980s dawned was the proposed extension of the U.S. Postal Service ZIP code from five decimal digits to some longer configuration. The problem, as a lot of people in the DP community saw it, was that all of their history files and their programs to process them would be obsoleted, and need revision to match the new ZIP configuration. If the DP people who took this position had had their way, the Postal Service would have been prohibited from making the change. (It is interesting to note that the DP community, riders of the waves of change and challenge that swept over the world in the middle of the twentieth century, have now arrived at the point where, from their entrenched position, they are the battlers against social change and innovation! Such is sometimes the way of social institutions that move from wedging their way into society in spite of its wishes, to being part of society's power structure.)

---

*McCracken, ACM President's Letter, Communications of the ACM, Vol. 21, no. 12, December 1978.

To at least some degree, the position of the DPers on the ZIP code was unreasonable. Computing is, in general, a service industry, whose goal is or should be to smooth other processes, making them easier or less costly or more feasible or some combination of the above. The fact that the difficulty of changing software to realign the ZIP code number, or to resynch the social security system, is a deterrent to those largely positive social changes is a serious commentary on the ability of the practitioners in our field to be flexible.

The lessons here are twofold—the importance of building software more flexibly in the first place, and the ability to innovate creatively within the constraints of an existing (flexible or nonflexible) system. The former is dealt with in section 3.2.2.1, where a variety of techniques for making software easier to change are discussed. The latter, however, falls not so much into the technical world of tools and methodologies, but into the people world of software practitioners.

The ability to innovate within constraints is a complex one. It requires the programmer to be accepting of the work of those who have gone before him, in order to retain as long as possible the mind-set that the software can be bent to fit the new requirements without the necessity of breaking it or throwing it away. It requires the programmer to have access to the whole spectrum of his thinking processes, to "brainstorm" his way to solutions that might not be traditional or compatible with his own stylistic approach. It requires the programmer to maintain a positive attitude through a taxing mental process, not giving in to the temptation to either quit in disgust or perform an exorbitantly expensive or crude brute-force solution.

These are subtle but vital requirements. They are highlighted here because, to an extent more visible than most other software processes, they have a significant impact on the ability of software to meet the needs of its customers. When the song of the Unsung Hero is being sung, here especially the chorus should swell. Those able to modify and innovate and create within the constraints placed on them not only by their management superstructure but also by their peers who have gone before them deserve a chorus or two all their own!

There are other constraints placed on the modifications to software. Not only is there an in-place product and an in-place management and peer structure—there are also external constraints that must be dealt with.

The customer's needs, one such constraint, will be discussed in the next section. If those needs are expressed in a contract, or perhaps less bindingly in a specification, they form a constraint that the maintainer must deal with.

Schedule, cost, and risk are another set of constraints. Often it will be true that if a modification cannot conform to specific schedule and/or cost constraints, it will not occur.

Reliability of the final product, discussed as a goal in the previous section, is also a constraint. If the modification threatens reliability, then in general it should not be made.

A peculiar form of feasibility also serves as a modification constraint. "Is the existing software product really compatible with the desired change?" is a question with constraint implications. If making the change would turn a finely tuned watch into a 20-year-old and battered Timex, the change should probably not be made. The maintainer must understand his product intimately to make that kind of judgment.

Finally, documentation, oddly enough, is often a constraint on modification. The cost of correcting, reissuing, and redistributing a document impacted by a change (e.g., the user's manual) may make it undesirable to make the change.

Juggling this long list of constraints is not the least of the problems of the Unsung Hero.

2.6   CUSTOMERS' NEEDS

The preceding sections open the door to another topic that deserves highlighting. To put it into proper focus, it is necessary to step back into computing's past a decade or two. Throughout the history of humankind, some occupations or avocations have received social accolades seemingly beyond their reasonable just desserts. One example, of course, is the sports or entertainment superstar, whose salary reward is so high as to be incomprehensible to more mundane folk who must earn a living with less flamboyant talents. Another, and more relevant, example are those careers that spark the imagination of the masses. At the juvenile level, firemen and policemen are the epitome of achievement. At a somewhat more mature level, the reporter or teacher captures the imagination and respect of the populace.

Computer programmers have, in the past, been a part of the latter category. As the manipulators of the omnipotent beasts who were moving, humanlike, to control society, the programmer was placed in a special niche. More relevant to our current topic, it felt good to be in that niche. Programmers loved and sometimes played on the respect and awe showered on them by a still-computer-naive public. But, the public has come to some more fundamental understandings of computers over the years. Computer types have become so common that over 70,000 of them frequently attend the national computing conferences, and almost everyone knows one personally by now. The awe is disappearing.

Left over from that awe, however, is sometimes the programmer's self-perception that his is a domain presided over only by himself. Managers have made severe inroads into that belief, with the principles of software engineering and management control moving ever closer to the programmers' inner sanctum. Still, it is true that no one but the programmer cares to look deep within the nitty-gritty details of the program product he is creating. Within that sanctum, the programmer is still in full control. Or is he?

Remember that every software system is built to satisfy some customer's need. Remember that every programming activity, even those labeled earlier as maintenance for maintenance sake, is performed with the goal in mind of serving the customer. It is vital for the programmer, even basking in his niche of leftover awe, to remember that his function and his goal is to produce a tool useful to his customer, not a thing of pristine but useless intellectual beauty. It may be best if the maintenance programmer thinks of his system as being the payroll program that writes his own paychecks. It probably is not, of course, and yet in a symbolic sense it always is. With this perspective it is a lot easier for the programmer to keep in mind that if the customer is not properly served, the programmer does not get paid!

A couple of anecdotes will put this into firmer perspective. One involves a programmer who believed that his company was about to lay him off. To thwart that move, he immediately began to build tricky and convoluted logic into his program, hoping that its complexity would make it so opaque to other programmers that he would have to be retained. He was obviously violating the principle of meeting the customer's needs first. And in a perverse form of self-fulfilling prophecy, he was, indeed, laid off [12]!

A more satisfying anecdote is the one about the programmer who found a way to merge his need to satisfy his customer with his own need to create an intellectually satisfying product. In this case, the program was one that mathematically simulated the combustion process of rocket propellants in order to analyze, without firing a rocket, what kind of thrust various propellants might produce. It was part of a customer process of optimizing the chemical makeup of rocket propellants. The programmer, knowing the customer's goals and seeing that they were thwarted by the limited number of chemical elements that the program could treat, found a way to modify the program to be able to accept any chemical additive that the customer might care to evaluate. The program became significantly and, in fact, uniquely more useful (no one had ever generalized that problem solution before), and the programmer felt a justifiable surge of pride akin to the awe in the niche.

Sometimes the customer's needs dictate otherwise-illogical actions. In this anecdote, the program in question produces a set of reports that control production activities in a shop. One set of reports tells the shop workers what actions to perform during their shift and in what order. Another set of reports tells production control personnel which parts are currently being manufactured in the shop and what their status and location are. The output of such a program obviously must be closely in tune with reality. At the point in time of the anecdote, a series of unfortunate but computer-typical circumstances had caused the reports to be late or erroneous two days out of the last five. The programmer of the story, realizing that the credibility of the program was at stake, deliberately froze the program at a workable level and refused to put in any more changes for a two-week period. For the programmer, it was a strange kind of self-imposed vacation—he deliberately avoided doing anything useful for two weeks! But for the program—and the customer—it was a vital time of stability. Sometimes for the sake of the customer's needs, doing nothing is better than doing something positive!

The anecdotes make it clear that serving the customer's needs is not a clear-cut, well-defined process. It is, rather, another instance where the maintenance programmer must be able to think innovatively and creatively to meet a goal which, in itself, is clear but whose achievement is not.

2.7   INDIVIDUAL RECOGNITION

The contrast between the team approach to software and the importance of the individual achiever has already been noted. There is one area, however, in which the impact of the individual should not be ignored, no matter how team-oriented the organization is. When a programmer develops a piece of software or its documentation, that person's name should be (semipermanently?) affixed to it. It is not simply a matter of giving credit where credit is due, although that is an important criterion. It is also a matter of affixing responsibility, and maintaining history.

Perhaps the best way to discuss this subject is by example. Suppose that Programmer A is a top-quality person whose only flaw is an inability to write cohesive documentation, whereas Programmer B documents like Steinbeck but designs and writes mediocre-at-best programs. In reading the maintenance manual for a program both A and B developed, it is worthwhile to know who designed which pieces. For one thing, a little subjective judgment may be superimposed over the words—a flowing discussion written by B may be discounted, or a clumsy-sounding description written by A probably does not mean that the corresponding code is equally clumsy. But far more important, it also identifies responsible people. If I don't understand A's writeup or B's code, I at least know who to go to for further information.

Such name-affixing should be done at the level of each page of documentation, and each module of code (and equally important for the same reasons, each entity should be dated). Then when the inevitable changes occur, it is easy to revise the name (and date) without traumatic change to the surrounding material.

These pragmatics should not obscure the basic fact that individual recognition, per se, is a worthy and desirable goal. It is one small but highly visible way of singing the song of the Unsung Hero!

2.8 REFERENCES

1. "Structured Programming in a Production Programming Environment," Proceedings of the IEEE International Conference on Reliable Software, 1975; Baker.

   Discusses structured coding and programming standards in the context of the structured programming methodology.

2. "BCS Software Production Data," RADC-TR-77-116, 1977; Black, Curnow, Katz, and Gray.

   Defines modern programming practices used at a software production company. Contrasts traditional programming practices with modern techniques; provides a thorough description and assessment of traditional style.

3. "The High Cost of Software," *Practical Strategies for Developing Large Software Systems,* Addison-Wesley, 1975; Boehm.

   Discusses the cost of software, and how that cost is broken down over the software-life-cycle phases. Sees coding as the least-cost item (compared to requirements definition, design, and testing).

4. *The Mythical Man-Month,* Addison-Wesley, 1975; Brooks.

   A treasury of insights into software management and software people, drawn from practical experience on the implementation of OS/360. Describes the role of the human being as an individual and as a team member in software development activities.

5. "Human Factors in Software Engineering," Computer, December 1979; a theme issue of the journal.

   Contains articles on human factors experiments in the software field. Authors (Schneiderman, Basili, Reiter, Gannon, and others) explore questions related to interactive system design, modern methodology benefits, and data reference frequency.

6. "Hints on Test Data Selection: Help for the Practicing Programmer," Computer, April 1978; DeMillo, Lipton, and Sayward.

   Makes a strong case for the use of an intuitive, ad hoc approach to testing, on the grounds that other approaches reject the truism that most programs under test are "nearly correct."

7. "The Humble Programmer" (1972 Turing Award Lecture), Communications of the ACM, 1972; Dijkstra.

Discusses the evolution of the programming profession. Stresses the
need for better and more reliable software methodologies. Uses a
humorous approach.

8.   "A Study of Fundamental Factors Underlying Software Maintenance
     Problems," ESD-TR-72-121, Vol. 11, 1971.

     A series of interviews with programmers on maintenance-relevant
     subjects. Also contains maintenance programmer diaries and case study
     reports.

9.   "The Paradigms of Programming," Communications of the ACM,
     August 1979; Floyd.

     Discusses the importance of underlying programming concepts in the
     evolution of software development. Calls them "paradigms" (the
     present book calls a subset of them "style"). This paper emerges from
     the 1979 Turing Award Lecture.

10. "The New Software Economics," Computerworld, January 8, 1979, and
     subsequent issues; Frank.

     Sees a new role for proprietary software products in the typical
     installation mix of software acquisition. Describes the future of
     software productivity improvement as "bleak." Says "the ultimate
     factor in software productivity is the capability of the individual
     software practitioner."

11. "Computing Breakthrough Becomes Breakdown," *The Universal Elixir
     and Other Computing Projects Which Failed,* Computing Trends,
     1977; Glass.

     Describes an attempt to use unskilled programmers for system software
     development.

12. *Software Reliability Guidebook,* Prentice-Hall, 1979; Glass.

     Surveys techniques for achieving software reliability. Discusses the
     interrelationship between reliability and maintenance. Describes a
     variety of tools and methodologies that can assist in making software
     more reliable.

13. Special Collection on Software Science, IEEE Transactions on Soft-
     ware Engineering, March 1979.

     Complexity, style, and maintenance of software are discussed in such
     papers as "Designing Software for Ease of Extension and Contraction,"

"Psychological Complexity of Software Maintenance," "Measuring Improvements in Program Clarity," and more.

14.   *The Elements of Programming Style,* McGraw-Hill, 1978; Kernighan and Plauger.

Presents a definition of good programming style by means of a set of about 100 rules augmented by examples and discussion. Elaborates such ideas as "Modularize—use subroutines," "Let the data structure the program," and "Don't comment bad code—rewrite it."

15.   "Staffing the Albatross Project," Datamation, February 1976; Kenney.

A facetious look at the problems of staffing a tightly budgeted and scheduled project.

16.   *Programmers and Managers—The Routinization of Computer Programming in the United States,* Springer-Verlag, 1977; Kraft.

Laments the "de-skilling" of the technologist in the large-project environment. Notes the "routinization" of the tasks performed previously by "creative and perhaps eccentric" people.

17.   *Programming Proverbs for Fortran Programmers,* Hayden, 1975; Ledgard.

Represents programming style as a series of "proverbs" or rules. This book contains Fortran rules; Ledgard has written other books for other languages.

18.   "Characteristics of Application Software Maintenance," UCLA Graduate School of Management, 1976; Lientz, Swanson, and Tompkins.

Surveys 69 computing installations to identify the characteristics of software maintenance. Studies largely COBOL-oriented environments with high ongoing maintenance needs.

19.   "Characteristics of Application Software Maintenance," Communications of the ACM, June 1978; Lientz, Swanson, and Tompkins.

An updating of [18].

20.   "First-Year Results from a Research Program on Human Factors in Software Engineering," Proceedings of the National Computer Conference, 1979; Love, Sheppard, Curtis, Milliman, and Borst.

Describes experiments into the factors affecting programmer efficiency and performance. Individual differences between programmers are seen as one important factor influencing performance.

21. *Reliable Software through Composite Design,* Petrocelli/Charter, 1975; Myers.

    Advocates modularity, if done properly, as the key to effective software development. Describes proper modularizing—how to design them, how to interrelate them. Stresses the importance of the design phase.

22. "Module Design and Coding," *Software Reliability,* Wiley–Interscience, 1976; Myers.

    Stresses the importance of high-level language. Also discusses structured coding, standards, and other coding techniques.

23. "A Controlled Experiment in Program Testing and Code Walkthroughs/ Inspections," Communications of the ACM, September 1978; Myers.

    Describes an experiment in error seeking using testing and code review. Sees these techniques as complementary, with both being necessary. Finds testing to be subject to considerable individual variability, and recommends using two independently operating testers.

24. "Research toward Ways of Improving Software Maintenance," ESD-TR-73-125, 1973; Overton, Colin, and Tillman.

    Describes an experiment in which software maintenance activities were measured. Contains many quotes from maintenance programmers. Stresses the structure ("conceptual groupings") of the software. Defines specific maintainability techniques, and a maintainability checklist. Discusses use of a graphics terminal to support maintenance.

25. "On the Criteria to Be Used in Decomposing Systems into Modules," Communications of the ACM, December 1972; Parnas.

    Uses an example to discuss two strategies for defining modules. Recommends modularizing to promote "information hiding," such that modules contain design decisions that are likely to change.

26. "The Influence of Software Structure on Reliability," Proceedings of IEEE International Conference on Reliable Software, 1975; Parnas.

    Distinguishes between reliability (delivering usable services) and correctness (meeting specifications). Emphasizes the importance of the former, and stresses modularizing to promote it. Poses questions pertinent to module definition.

27. "Comparing Software Design Methodologies," Datamation, November 1977; Peters and Tripp.

Presents and analyzes five different design approaches. Evaluates the approaches based on trial usage. Concludes that no single approach is valid for all problems, and that "designers produce designs, methods do not."

28.   "Notes on the Design of Euclid," Proceedings of an ACM Conference on Language Design for Reliable Software, 1977; Popek, Horning, Lampson, Mitchell, and London.

Describes a language for writing system programs, called Euclid, which stresses capabilities for verification. Contains a good discussion on the Euclid philosophy of module/cluster definition.

29.   "Higher Order Languages for Avionics Software—A Survey, Summary and Critique," NAECON 1978; Rubey.

Traces the history of avionics (real-time) HOL usage. Cites problems and resolutions in HOL versus assembler trade-offs. Sees trends leading toward more HOL usage, but stresses that "the programmer's experience is a major factor in achieving high efficiency."

30.   Letter to the Editor, SIGPLAN Notices, December 1978; Soroka.

Suggests that people have characteristic programming styles, and that further research into the subject is needed.

31.   *Program Style, Design, Efficiency, Debugging and Testing*, Prentice-Hall, 1974; Van Tassel.

Contains a compilation of "programming lore" derived from software experience.

32.   *The Psychology of Computer Programming*, Van Nostrand Reinhold, 1971; Weinberg.

Discusses "egoless programming" and individual ownership of programs. Advocates the team approach to software development and reviews. Uses an anecdotal approach.

33.   "The Programming Language Pascal," Acta Information, 1, 1971; Wirth.

Presents the Pascal language—its capabilities and form.

34.   "An Assessment of the Programming Language Pascal," Proceedings of the International Conference on Reliable Software, June 1975; Wirth.

Evaluates the Pascal language.

35.   "Modula: A Language for Modular Multiprogramming," Software Practice and Experience, 2, 1, 1977; Wirth.

Describes the Pascal-based language Modula, which is intended for writing system software for small computers. Companion articles describe the use, design, and implementation of the language.

36.   *Software Psychology,* Winthrop, 1980; Shneiderman.

A definitive study on people who build software, this book has sections on programming style, team organization, and personality factors.

Three

The Technical Side
of Maintenance

Software systems may be thought of as living beings. How viable they are in performing their intended function is dependent on their nurturing and upbringing, in the same fashion as a child. The material in this section deals with the technical approaches to nurturing good software.

If you are reading this section to get an answer to the question "How can I reduce my maintenance costs?" and the question is about an already mature system, you may be asking the question too late. The nurturing and upbringing of the system have already determined its complexity, its modifiability, and therefore to a large extent its maintenance cost. Ask, instead, about your *next* software system. And then learn enough about how to nurture software to make the answer to the question come out the way you want it to.

This is not to say that there is no help for the mature system. By a process of evolution, it is possible to use the ideas of this section to change a difficult-to-modify system into a not-so-difficult-to-modify system. But like the nurturing of a child, it is best to begin the correct nurturing process early.

As we have seen in the preceding sections, the goals and priorities of the maintainer are fairly well defined. This section will attempt to explore in more detail the mechanics of how the goals are achieved. We will also see that the technical resources of maintenance will be consumed in ways not strictly defined as one of the maintainer's goals. In order to accomplish the task of maintenance, there is a framework within which the maintainer must operate. That framework consists of the user requirements, the existing program, the tools available, the environment, and the maintainer's own capabilities.

The maintainer has a responsibility to the entire software product. The most obvious application of maintenance resources is in the execution of the software itself. However, the entire software product is the proper object of maintenance. User's manuals often contain errors, ambiguities, and oversights that cause difficulty for the user. Correcting the up-front documents will consume a good portion of the maintainer's time. Documenting problems and potential improvements is necessary to keep users apprised of the true condition of the software. The specifications of the software may contain ambiguities and errors. It is part of the function of the maintainer to point these out and cause resolution of the difficulties.

The maintainer is faced, then, with a diverse set of tasks. All of these tasks can be performed manually and by ad hoc methodologies. In fact, historically most of them have been. However, as the Big Business of software grows bigger, it is becoming more and more obvious that the programmer must employ the best of his own technology on his own tasks. The best of the technology is the discipline of systems analysis and the convenience of automation. Systems analysis leads to better technologies, and automation leads to better tools. Those technologies and tools are the subject of this section.

Before moving into a discussion of the technologies and tools available to the maintainer, we will pause briefly to analyze the maintainer's job. In the true spirit of systems analysis, this will constitute a requirements definition for the technologies and tools solutions to follow.

3.1   WHAT THE MAINTAINER DOES

Part of the difficulty of a manager's job supervising a maintenance programmer is that he often doesn't really know what the maintainer is doing. In this section we attempt to present a somewhat chronological description of the things involved in the maintenance task. We look at the entire gamut of the maintenance task for one idealized problem. If you multiply this process many times and interweave the parts dynamically, you may begin to appreciate just how much is really being accomplished.

The maintainer usually spends a great deal of time analyzing the raw data of suspected problems. The process often starts with the approach of a somewhat disgruntled user. Great differences can exist even at this point, depending on the type of software system being maintained. For example, a payroll program user can say with a great deal of certainty: "These numbers don't match! The program has a bug." On the other hand, a compiler user might say: "My program is acting strangely. Could there be a bug in the compiler?"

In order to winnow out the real program errors from the things that look like errors (but are *possibly* something else), the maintenance programmer will probably have to spend a significant part of the time making these distinctions. During this time, he will attempt to form some kind of opinion about the problem and its probable cause. He may ask many questions of the user; he might use several reference works, such as user's manuals, program specifications, maintenance documents, and program listings to ferret out some obscure operation of the program, or to come to a working hypothesis. During this time he must be concerned with the search for truth; that is, is this a user problem; is it a shortcoming in the program, whereby it is operating correctly but maybe not very clearly; is it a question of unclear documentation; or is it really a program problem? Consider, also, that this initial contact with a potential problem may well come at the worst possible moment.

The maintainer has been deeply involved in the solution of another problem when interrupted, and the newcomer blithely asks, "Have you got a minute?" Enough to blow even a very heavy-duty fuse!

Well, you have sent away an earlier questioner with a reasonable explanation of what happened, with a promise (and some hastily scribbled notes) to improve the user's manual. But this new customer has really got something. After 20 minutes of conversation and looking at supplementary data, you both agree that something is definitely wrong. You reach for your pad of Problem Reports and start documenting the failure. The customer is crestfallen! "You mean you can't fix this in 20 minutes?" They never say it, of course; but you can recognize that look on their face. After a few minutes thought, you dream up some kind of work-around that they might use. You jot down the work-around on the Problem Report (in case somebody else finds the same problem), and *voila!* another moderately happy customer goes on his way.

Assuming that you have a fairly continuous stream of these reasons for your existence, you frequently will find yourself performing another bit of analysis. This one is called "Let's go through the list of problems and assign priorities" or "What should I work on next?" Often, you will have a great deal of assistance in this job. All of the problem-finders you spoke to in the last month wander by occasionally to ask if you have their problem fixed, and to review the entire process again, or merely to point out that they are really "hung-up" by their problem. So this task is not nearly as tedious as it might be. You do have lots of help!

Now you have some time to really fix problems. (You came in at 10:30 on Saturday evening, because it's nice and quiet.) From the top of your nicely prioritized stack, you grab problem report HOTTEST. You reach into the stack of "substantiating documentation" (user's listing), which you have numbered to correspond with the problem report. You drag out the dog-eared listing of the "offending program" and the user's manual and the specification and the maintenance documentation, and with this tidy little pile of material, you go to work. You read a little here and you diagram a little there and you look up over here and repeat this process several times and in just no time at all (it goes quickly when you're having fun), you have identified the offending piece of code. Possibly.

Now, we'll try a little solution on it. All it takes is this little change here and that should do it.

Let's digress for just a moment. If all of the programs were written by "ideal" programmers and the documentation accurately reflected every concept and idea he originally had (even those he discarded), and the programs were beautiful, and "modular" and "structured" and simple and straightforward, and human errors such as transpositions and misplaced lines of code and minor test discrepancies and so forth never happened, maintenance would be a breeze. But the real world isn't like that. Most programs have "evolved" to their present state. They have grown and been "kludged" and been expedited. As a result, getting to the place where our "little fix" is appropriate is oftentimes not very easy. And in fact the "little fix" is often not easy either.

Anyhow, back to the problem and its solution. We've got the "fix." Our work must be done. Not so! Now comes some quality assurance work. The maintainer must now test the corrected system. In many cases, the system will have a series of test cases which will give some indication of the quality of the entire system, but most often the individual problems that require correction in the system do not have a test case. The generalized solution is therefore to add a test for the specific problem to the existing tests. A little dab more of "nonproductive" time added to the cost of maintenance. Run the test, run the standardized "regression" tests, and turn out the new product. Easy? Yes, sometimes. Sometimes a little poke in the fabric here causes a stretch over there. Reexamine and resolve the problem. Eventually it works! Is maintenance finished here? *No.* Documentation updates, release notices, problem report closures still have to be accomplished. The maintenance programmer's work, like that in the cliché, is never done.

3.1.1   The Maintainer and the User

For an individual in a maintenance role, large portions of his time will be spent, as we have already seen in this section, answering questions, sifting out potential problems, analyzing requirements and specifications, and even helping with problems not directly related to the maintenance task. It must be recognized that the user of a system is not always very well versed in its use, whereas the maintainer is probably very knowledgeable about what the system can do. One of two methods is available to the training of users. Either they are (1) formally trained in a classroom environment in the use of the system, or (2) they are given ongoing consultation support. Both may in fact be necessary. The maintainer may end up playing one or both of those roles.

In addition, the maintainer may either be situated in the same physical location as the users, or he may be made very remote. Those who are extremely accessible for consultation will be accessed. Those who are remote will also be accessed, but much less frequently.

In any case, the maintainer becomes an added resource for the user. His knowledge and expertise can be called upon to provide another dimension to the user of the software product. But note that another bite is thereby taken out of the maintenance dollar and the maintainer's time.

3.1.2   The Maintainer and the Problem Report

Software problems may be broken down into two categories, old and new. Let us take first the handling of a new problem. A method of keeping track of each problem as reported should be developed. The description of the problem is added to a problem report data base (manually or preferably in some automated form). Many potential problems can be quickly resolved by reference to the report containing the list of known problems.

The problem description must be detailed from two different standpoints: the user's, providing a reasonable understanding of what the problem is, and a method of working around it; and the program's, showing what went wrong and a probable cause. All this information may require some amount of analysis to gather. Backup documentation may be necessary and some method of filing the data together with the supporting information will be required.

In any case, formal reporting of problems is a must. That subject is discussed in more depth in section 4.2.2.

3.2   HOW THE MAINTAINER DOES IT

This section will take a look at the tools and techniques that a maintainer uses or could use to perform his function. The tools (automated methods) we look at include both the traditional software with which a development programmer operates, and some unique to the maintainer's needs. The techniques (primarily manual methods) emerge from accumulated years of programming experience, and include some methods for applying them.

3.2.1   Tools

Maintenance, as has been seen, is a large portion of the software life cycle. It, as much or more than any phase of software development, is all too often left out of planning considerations. The software industry has, as one of its prime functions, assisting in the increasing use of computers to replace and/or serve the human effort to perform a given task. But to a large extent, the software business does not use the computer to aid in its own task.

It must be recognized that a "system" is going to exist for what often turns out to be a long but finite period (for some programs, this seems to approach infinity). The necessity for maintenance must be also recognized and planned for.

Does there exist a significant piece of software, anywhere, which was turned over to the ultimate user and which was never found to be in error or require modification? In spite of sometimes flamboyant claims to the contrary, the correct answer is "hardly ever."

The fact of errors and the longevity of maintenance demands that long-term planning be applied. That long-term planning, just as in other disciplines, includes the provision of appropriate tools. It is time for the software builder and maintainer to use tools—including computerized ones—to improve the performance of his job. The day when a dump was the only required maintenance tool has passed. We need more expressive and more productive methods of evaluating our problems. (A good elementary-level discussion of the notion of tools is found in ref. [23].)

There are two major categories of tools that are required for the maintenance task. The first of these has to do with the technical side of the task. These tools include compilers, assemblers, linkage editors, operating systems, debugging tools, traps and traces, dumps, symbolic printouts, levels analysis, comparators, test coverage analyzers, verification tools, validation tools, test cases, cross-reference listings, text editors, reformatters, and preprocessors.

The second category of tools enables the maintainer to carry out his administrative functions. The processes include problem reporting, status reporting, change review, documentation, and recording historical perspectives.

Both of these sets of tools can be run in either a batch mode (user submits jobs and returns later for output) or in an interactive timesharing mode (the user interacts with programs, usually via a hardcopy or CRT terminal). The methods used will be somewhat different, primarily because of the time lag of the batch process.

It is the authors' recommendation that the interactive mode be used whenever possible because of the tremendous increase in productivity it brings about. This recommendation, it must be acknowledged, is unfortunately ahead of the maintenance state of the art as practiced at most computing installations.

There are, of course, some advantages and disadvantages to use of the interactive mode. The advantages are potent—the maintainer can accomplish in a short session on the terminal what would normally require several batch turnarounds, which in many computing installations is equated to several days. His thought patterns are not interrupted by the delay of waiting for turnaround. Disadvantages do exist, however. The batch maintainer usually performs other tasks, such as documentation, between turnarounds. Therefore, the total productivity improvement is not as great as the debug productivity improvement. More seriously, the maintainer may tend to make snap judgments on program revisions at the terminal rather than taking the time to redesign a change before its implementation. Discipline is needed to inhibit this kind of diddling.

Still, the net gain of interactive mode has been verified fairly consistently in experimental studies. The recommendation above may be soundly justified [43, 47]. More generally, it should be stressed that the scarcest resource in software development is the understanding brain. Tools that improve brain productivity, such as timesharing, are essential.

3.2.1.1   TOOLS FOR MAINTENANCE ITSELF

The tools that follow are the ones the maintainer needs to do his job. They directly assist in the maintenance of the software product.

Language

One of the most important decisions to be made with regard to a software system is the choice of language. The specification of language is not generally within the realm of maintenance, but consideration of the impact of language choice must include the role that maintenance will play. We strongly advocate the use of the highest-order language possible for both design and implementation work.

The subject of design representation is dealt with later in this section. It is important to note here, however, that the design representation—more and more often, these days, a program design language—should be chosen with a number of expressive capabilities in mind:

1. System-to-subsystem decomposition.
2. Interface specification, both external and internal.
3. Data structure definition, and system data flow.
4. Algorithm and control structure expression.

Perhaps more important, especially from the point of view of this discussion, the design representation should be:

5. Compatible with the chosen programming language.
6. Insertable into the program as commentary.

The latter two criteria, especially, make the design language a preferred form of design representation. Older techniques, such as flow charting, are at their worst in the maintenance phase since they are difficult to modify and are often, therefore, out of date.

Not only do we advocate the use of high-level design and implementation languages, but also their consistent use throughout a software system. All too often, different parts of a system are coded in different languages. The result is not really a system at all.

The bulk of a system may pay lip service to the use of a single language for all design and programming, but without strong management, the number of languages involved in the system soon proliferates. In many cases, some parts of the system are concluded to be inappropriate for use of the "official" language and exceptions are granted for use of other languages.

The primary culprit here is the introduction of assembly language instead of high-order language (HOL). The usual guise that brings this one forth is efficiency. For example, "the compiler does not produce efficient code for these particular functions so we need to do them in assembly language."

The second intrusion into the common HOL use is made by the lack of training. Programmers are put on the project who do not have experience with the language being used. In some fashion, and with the concurrence of management, they are allowed to use another HOL or assembly language for some portion of the programming task.

Then, too, in the area of support tools for the system, implementation of these tools themselves is not thought to be part of the system, and sometimes tool-builders are allowed to stray from the language requirements. Particularly here, we see ad hoc tools created that were overlooked by the original design and thus are not officially part of the system. These are often categorized as "nondeliverables" and so fall outside the project controls and thus are frequently written in a different language.

For all these reasons, it is not unusual to see a "system" that consists of many programs being maintained in four or five different languages.

Consider now the maintenance of this so-called system. *This* program requires "specialized knowledge" (read "a different language") to correct. Good discussions of the importance of HOLs are found in refs. [3, 41, 42, 46, 58, and 59].

It is worth noting that a language is not a useful tool to the software maintainer without a language processor. That subject is dealt with in the next section.

The Language Processor (Compiler)

The most widespread, necessary and sometimes the only maintenance tool in existence currently is the language processor [2, 41].

Every piece of software exists as a "mental image." The customer has specified a task to be performed. The designer has given a shape to the image by specifying, in detail, the various parts of the task and the interfaces between them. Someone has levied a requirement for the language to be used in solving the problem. Someone has determined the particular computer to be used. Some developer has "created" his solution to the task. The many constraints levied upon the software are epitomized in the program. How well the program performs its task is dependent on the judgments of (usually) many people.

Whether it is solved in terms of a highly structured HOL or a set of machine instructions, the program ultimately exists in the form of

The Language Processor (Compiler)

INPUT	PROCESSING	OUTPUT

1. Application program(s) written in some programming language.	2. Translation, programming language to computer language.	1. Object code version of application program(s).
		 2. Listing of source program, augmented by
		   a. Appropriate headings, including language processor version identification, time/date of compilation, name of program.
		   b. Line numbering.
		   c. Diagnostics for source errors.
		   d. Cross-reference listing.
		   e. Memory map.
		   f. Processor summary, including memory allocated, external references, resources used during compilation.
		 3. Files needed by interfacing tools, if any.

Example of Usage: A program written in Ada is input to a compiler executing on the VAX computer. The output is to be an object program for the Z8000 microcomputer, and the supporting listings. All output will be produced on the VAX.

source code, which is acted upon by a *language processor* which turns the source code into an executing program and a *listing.* Since the sequence of instructions that are followed in performance of the task exist in the form of the listing, it is usually thought of by experienced programmers as the embodiment of the program. When corrections are to be made, they are generally made to the listing. This may exist as paper or may only be in the form of images on a CRT.

To a large extent, the language processor is called upon to provide most of the information that the programmer needs about the program itself. The function of the language and its compiler is to remove the attention of the programmer from the details of manipulating the computer, freeing him to concentrate on the solution of the problem.

Compilers and languages must provide access not only to the logical facilities needed for problem solving but also to the services that are potentially provided by an operating system (OS). Normally, input/output is provided in at least rudimentary form by all languages, but more advanced types of data manipulation must also be made available through the language. The types of services include almost all OS-type capabilities, such as time of day, requests for resources, activity synchronization, and so on. All too often in the environment of current languages, requests of this type must be performed via direct interface with the operating system, usually by the use of assembly language, which again forces the programmer to deal with unnecessary details.

Current language processors provide no more than rudimentary information about the program being processed. These usually take the form of a cross-reference listing (an alphabetized list of all names, showing where they are set and used), and sometimes a map (a memory-ordered listing of variables). These lists, although rudimentary, are essential for the maintainer to do his job.

Information that could be provided by the language processor, in addition to that currently produced, might include the following:

Procedure-oriented cross-reference listing. The most common *cross-reference* programs currently output their information by relating variable usage to the statement numbers in the program. This information is important, but it is also the minimum necessary to be of any use. Far better than statement number, for example, would be to output the information based on named entities in the program. Which named procedure set or used a variable would be far more descriptive than which statement number set or used a variable. The named procedures that called or were called by a given procedure would provide much more information than the statement number where a procedure was called.

Some of this information is currently being produced by preprocessors or postprocessors to the compilation process, but they are really in the realm of duties that can easily be, and should be, performed by the language processor itself.

Data structure reference listing. Another function that might be provided by the compiler, and which is of particular importance in certain environments, is the *data structure reference listing*. A data structure is an aggregate of data where not only the whole aggregate is named, but constituent elements are named as well. Where a data structure is accessed or modified via its constituent names, the ability to extract these references, together with some knowledge of the environment in which they occur, is extremely important. A list, for each structure, of all its references—especially in the procedure-oriented manner described previously—would be extremely useful.

Linkage Editors

INPUT	PROCESSING	OUTPUT
1. Processed source modules produced by the language processor.	1. Allocate object programs to computer memory for loading purposes. 2. Resolve external references by binding library and other external modules into the allocated program.	1. Ready to load and execute program.

Example of Usage: Object modules for software system PAYROLL are input to the linkage editor on the CYBER computer, together with control information describing where in the data base supporting library routines may be found. The linkage editor assigns the complete program to CYBER memory and produces a module that can be loaded and executed.

The *linkage editor* typically provides the means to piece together the programs in the system. Its function is to provide access at an intraprogram level, satisfying *external* definitions and preparing programs for execution.

However, all too frequently, contemporary linkage editors impose limitations on the programmer. For example, traditional linkage editors often restrict the user to six- or eight-character external names. This practice dates back to the era when Fortran and assembler were the only languages a linker had to support. With modern languages facilitating much longer, more readable names—the kind the maintainer most desperately needs—it is a peculiar bottleneck that the linker creates in not supporting them. This inadequacy needs to be removed. Fortunately, the new Department of Defense triservices programming language, Ada, requires a linker whose name capability is consistent with those of the language [41]. Thus, this archaic bottleneck may at last be in the process of being abolished.

Needed also at the linker level is the capability of cross-referencing all system-known names (not just the external ones). Obviously, it is conceptually possible for a linker to collect and process compiler-produced symbol tables from separate compilations in order to produce a truly comprehensive cross-reference. Rarely, however, has this been done.

Still another function that could be performed by the linker, but seldom is, is consistency checking of parameter lists. Is the calling routine using the same call sequence that the called routine expects? For external routines, only the linker can provide this check. (For the previously mentioned Ada language, this may not be true. It is required there that the language provide control on these kinds of consistency checks, and thus a more powerful compiler will commonly play this role.) Whatever the case, this checking also has not traditionally been performed.

Thus, we have the link edit tool—vitally useful to the maintainer, but woefully archaic in its evolution to meet his needs.

Operating System/Executive

Operating system or executive programs are usually delivered with the computer hardware, and provide a logical machine upon which the application programs run and by means of which they communicate

INPUT	PROCESSING	OUTPUT

1. Application programs and systems to be executed.	1. Computer hardware-intimate services are provided to the application programs.
	  a. Scheduling.
	  b. Resource sharing.
	  c. Interrupt servicing.
		1. Properly executed application programs.

Example of Usage: System PAYROLL is loaded into the CYBER computer for execution. The CYBER's operating system schedules it for execution, initiates that execution, provides it with input-output services, gives control to other executing programs when PAYROLL's execution is waiting for resources, and tidies up when it completes execution.

with the physical machine. They provide many services to the user programs.

The distinction between an "operating system" and an "executive" usually depends on the use of the system. *Operating systems* are generally used when the computer performs a general-purpose role: many users with different requirements for computational ability. The services provided are generally resource management, data management, and task management. The "language" used to communicate to the operating system is crude, low-level, and usually very different from the user's HOL or even assembly language.

The same or similar functions provided in a dedicated (usually real-time) environment are called *executives.* The executive is usually tailored to a specific application. Although there is no real conceptual difference between an operating system and an executive, in practice they may turn out to be significantly different pieces of software, because of the application needs.

Of prime importance to the software maintainer is the method whereby the operating system/executive provides services to the using world. Between any two different computers and their operating system are apt to be vast differences in the way these capabilities are provided. It should not be necessary for the user to think of the physical connection to the operating system; and the details of interrupt drivers, stacking and queueing, buffering, and so on, should be removed from the user. What he requires is convenient access to the functions that he needs to perform his problem solution. The degree to which that goal is met determines to a large extent the convenience the maintainer finds in living with maintenance changes that impact operating system interfaces. Frequently, maintainability of software demands that such interfaces be isolated into identifiable application program modules, such that if change is necessary, only that module need to be changed.

Built-in Debug Tools

INPUT	PROCESSING	OUTPUT

1. Indications of debug data to be gathered during program execution, such as
  a. Data traces.
  b. Logic traces.
  c. Anomalous results.
	1. Print data gathered in human-readable form.	1. Printout of requested data, either interspersed with normal program output or in a separate file:
		  a. Variable names and their values.
		  b. Indications of program logic elements executed.
		  c. Diagnostics for anomalous results.

Examples of Usage: The Ada program compiled earlier did not execute properly under test. The programmer inserts into the source code, using conditional compilation, debug commands to trace variables ALPHA and BETA, and all procedure entries. He also specifies the range of BETA and GAMMA, and asks that any time values outside that range are created that a range diagnostic be produced. When the program is compiled (with conditional compilation "on") and linked and executed again, support routines are provided to produce the requested trace output and diagnostics. The programmer receives some debug results to help him isolate the problem.

Any large program should have the capability of reporting information about its own internal states. Most general-purpose tools are incapable of providing the kind of information required in a suitable format for immediate use in solving problems. Some large percentage of any program, then, should provide specialized means by which the maintainer can look at data within the program. These specialized means can simply be print statements for key variables, a more generally defined trace mechanism invoked for certain variables, or even assertions whose status is printed only when they are untrue (e.g., when SIZE $\leq$ 100 is not true).

Obviously, normal use of the program will not require the execution of this built-in debug capability. In fact, in a real-time system, the extra time and space required for the debug code may not be desirable. The maintainer, however, should have the ability during a subsequent debug run to produce additional analyses to aid in the solution of the problem [35, 41].

Typically, this capability is provided by a routine that prints out the required data in a symbolic form (e.g., VELOCITY = 55). This routine is controlled by a parameter easily accessible to the programmer. In ordinary uses of the program, this control parameter would have a default value of "off." When the maintainer needs the information, he simply submits the same job, with the control parameter "on."

It should seldom be necessary to physically remove debug code. Conditional compilation techniques allow the inclusion or exclusion of source text in the compilation by control code. Debug code can simply be keyed to such a code and left in the program.

Some recent systems (e.g., [17]) allow symbolic debug interaction with a program without requiring preplanned debug code. The systems are powerful enough that they can provide services when the need arises. However, until such systems are in widespread use, preplanning is essential to good debugging.

The recommendation here is that one-fourth to one-third of every large program consist of built-in symbolic debugging code. This recommendation is rarely met, in practice. Here again, the needs of the maintainer are frequently given short shrift in the development process.

Comparator

There are many situations in the maintenance field where comparators are extremely useful. A *comparator* is a program that takes two sets of information and summarizes, in a useful form, the differences between them. Some very obvious applications of this technique are:

INPUT	PROCESSING	OUTPUT
1. Two files whose content are to be compared.	1. Compare files for identicality. When content is not identical, compensate for differences to keep files in synchronization.	1. Print indication of file mismatches: contents of both files when they differ.

Examples of Usage: The version of PAYROLL run today produces different results from the one executed last month. The source code for both versions is read into a comparator and a listing of differences is produced.

comparisons of two source programs, test-case comparisons (regression tests), and test-result comparisons.

One of the criteria for operation of this tool is that the two sets of data be similar enough to provide a meaningful measure of their differences. Comparing apples and oranges almost never bore any fruit. (Is this metaphor a lemon?)

The ability to compare two different versions of the same program, obtaining a concise listing of those differences, will be immediately useful to the maintainer. A common question asked of a maintainer is: "What is the (operational) difference between version X and version Y of this program?" Another is: "This program used to work, and now it doesn't. Precisely what is different about it?" Comparators readily help to answer these kinds of questions.

A second area where comparators are useful is in test-result or "regression" analysis. The maintainer executes two different versions of his program with the same test data and captures the results of execution of the two versions. He is interested in ascertaining all the places where there are differences brought about by this change so that they may be checked for appropriateness.

In both of the cases described above, the desired form of the output must be related somehow to the type of data input. That is, in comparing source listings, for example, what we would wish to have is a side-by-side listing of the source, with differences noted; or simply an exception list of differences. Simple differences such as card sequence numbers, which are probably not meaningful, might be optionally ignored by the comparator; but the content of source lines is the important difference and should be clearly noted. It would be nice if reformatting of a source line could be reported on option only. In any case, the differences to be reported and those to be ignored should be easily specifiable.

The problems in the creation of a comparator are: first, we must have either a very "smart" general-purpose comparator or we may instead spawn a host of them, one for every type of comparison we might wish to make. Second, attention must be given to resynchronizing the comparison process so that an early mismatch does not cause everything that follows to be shown as a mismatch. Third, the tool, as all tools, must be reasonably economical to use.

Fortunately, these goals are met in commercially available products. The FILCOM program on the Digital Equipment Corp. DEC10, for one example, is a general-purpose tool which, especially for source files (programs, test cases, test results, etc.), does a good job of giving an exception report of differences while recovering from synchronization problems.

Given files consisting of the data

A
B
C
D
E
F

and

A
B
D
F1

for example, FILCOM would produce this output:

1) C
1) D
***
2) D
********** (showing that C is missing from file 2)

1) E
1) F
***
2) F1
********** (showing that E and F are missing from file 2 and that
            file 2 contains F1)

Text Editor

INPUT	PROCESSING	OUTPUT

1. Text.
2. Commands to ma-
nipulate text.
	1. Perform requested commands on the text:
	  a. Delete infor-
	    mation.
	  b. Insert infor-
	    mation.
	  c. Replace infor-
	    mation.
	  d. Print infor-
	    mation.
		1. Text modified as specified by the commands.

Example of Usage: Variable BETA in one module of an Ada program is erro-
neously exported to a module containing a different variable BETA. In addition, the
initial value of BETA is set incorrectly. A text editor is used to replace all references to BETA in the second program's source code to BETA_LOCAL, and to
change the initial value of BETA as needed.

Since the embodiment of any program is the source code representation of that program, and since the maintenance of the program
requires changing the source code, one of the most necessary tools is a
text editor. Via a text editor, text may be supplemented, deleted, or
revised. The most rudimentary form of editors operate upon a single
line of source, allowing single records to be inserted or deleted. The use
of these tools is about equivalent to requiring a mechanic to fix a car
using only a crescent wrench. When it is necessary to change a single
character in one line, the entire line must be reinserted, thereby
introducing the possibility of further errors. Text or source code
editors must be simple to use, powerful, and again should be
interactive with the user. Segments of code should be movable with a
simple command. A sequence of code repeated many times throughout

a program should be replaceable by another sequence by one command. Inadvertent side-effect errors should be minimized and flagged with warning messages, where possible.

Even the simplest text editors available today tend to have the following kinds of capabilities:

1. Line-oriented (the line to be impacted is specified)
   a. Delete
   b. Insert
   c. Replace
   d. Print
2. String-oriented (the string to be impacted is specified)
   a. Find
   b. Substitute
3. Block-oriented (the block of lines to be impacted is specified)
   a. Copy
   b. Replace

Almost any source code manipulation the maintenance programmer may need is achievable by these kinds of capabilities. For example, one might use a text editor, during an edit session on a program being maintained, to

1. Replace a line of code with a corrected line of code (replace).
2. Insert three additional lines of new code (insert).
3. Change all references to the variable named RMS to ROOT-MEAN-SQUARE (substitute).
4. Locate all references to procedure DIAGNOSTIC for further analysis (find).
5. Save both the old and new versions of the program (copy).

Some text editors provide even more sophistication, such as the ability to write "programs" of command strings, where each command in the program performs one of the capabilities named above. With added sophistication sometimes comes added risk—such a program can make profound changes to a source text—both profound good and profound bad! In spite of such risk, a powerful text editor may well be the maintainer's best friend. Programmers have been known to become very enthusiastic about their favorite editors.

Again, fortunately, most computer vendors now supply such products with their hardware. Especially in the timesharing environment, good text editors are commonly available and used.

Reformatter

INPUT	PROCESSING	OUTPUT
1. Text.	1. Format the text to improve its readability. A set of predefined readability rules is used.	1. Text modified by the readability rules.

Example of Usage: The changes to PAYROLL to correct it for last month's error were inserted hastily and hamper program readability. The reformatter is invoked to produce a better-indented, more readable version of the PAYROLL source.

As languages become better structured, the importance of a good, readable indentation scheme increases. That comment may be considered obscure without an example. Consider the readability of the following two code sequences:

```
(a) for I in 1.. FILE_TABLE_SIZE loop
        if FILE_TABLE(I) = FILE_NAME then return I; end if:
        if FILE_TABLE(I) = NULL then
            FILE_TABLE(I): = FILE_NAME; return I; end if;
    end loop;
(b) for I in 1.. FILE_TABLE_SIZE loop if
    FILE_TABLE(I) = FILE_NAME then return I;
    end if; if FILE_TABLE(I) = NULL then
    FILE_TABLE(I): = FILE_NAME; return I;
    end if; end loop;
```

The content of both sequences is identical, but the format of the first is readable, whereas the second is not.

It is easy for the programmer to provide this kind of indentation, and most programmers do. However, for those who do not, for those who maintain programs written by those who did not, and for those using a timesharing system with inadequate tabbing (indentation) capability, it may be desirable to have a tool to perform an automated indentation. Such a tool is called a *reformatter* (or, sometimes, a "prettyprinter"). Obviously, the tool contains a set of rules defining which elements of program structure should be indented, and how. This concept will be dealt with in a different context in section 3.2.2.1.

Flowcharts and Program Design Languages (PDLs)

INPUT	PROCESSING	OUTPUT

1. Design in computer-readable form:
  a. Flow chart—program text augmented with flow information commentary.
  b. PDL—program-like text.
	1. Flow chart—prepare flow graphics output.
	2. PDL—consistency-check design.
		1. Flow chart—graphic version of input design.
		2. PDL—reformatted design with consistency check results.

Examples of Usage: a. Following its modification, PAYROLL's flow chart is now obsolete. The flow charter is invoked to produce a new and correct version. b. The modification of BETA in the Ada program still doesn't correct the problem. There appears to be a design error. The PDL processor is used on the program's source code (which contains the PDL design as commentary) to produce a design listing and a cross-reference showing all design references to BETA.

Flowcharts have been the traditional means for representing program design. With the advent of powerful HOLs, the need or utility of flowcharts has been superseded. The only use that the authors have found for flowcharts is as quick and dirty design aids, and as a form for extracting the design of an existing program (the flowchart can be used to doublecheck the validity of the program). As with other forms of separate documentation, unless the flowchart physically corresponds to the source listing, it is useless. Because of the inherent difficulty of keeping flowcharts up to date, most maintenance programmers simply ignore them, going instead to the listing for the information they need.

Preferable forms of design representation are evolving. (For a humorous treatment of this evolution, see ref. [15].) The *program design language* (PDL) is especially promising. Particularly when the PDL is inserted in the program code as commentary, the accuracy of this nongraphic representation is more likely to be trusted by the maintainer seeking to understand the code it describes. As previously mentioned in the discussion of languages, the PDL should in fact be compatible with the coding language, both from the point of view that the general form be similar, and from the point of view that it be consistent with the coding language commentary rules.

Inclusion of the design representation in the code means that the design will not get lost, as has traditionally happened. The maintainer, in his mini-life-cycle need to analyze requirements and do design and implement code, will now have the original design readily and accurately available as a maintenance starting place.

Tools are often used to support both of these methodologies. For the flowchart, the tool extracts information from a program and produces the flowchart graphics for it. (Such tools are often not terribly useful unless they rely on the programmer to insert flowchart commentary into the program to help describe what is being done.) PDL tools read a PDL much like a compiler reads a program, and produce (1) consistency checks of the PDL (are any design elements missing? redundant?); (2) cross-referencing of the PDL; and (3) a listing of the design itself. The existence of the PDL tool is a relatively new development in the programmer's toolbox.

Verification Aids

INPUT	PROCESSING	OUTPUT
1. Program needing verification. 2. Test cases or criteria.	1. Program executed as specified by test cases or as manipulated by criteria.	1. Program execution results. 2. Anomalous results. 3. Analysis of execution/anomalous results.

Example of Usage: Someone asks if PAYROLL has ever been verified to execute correctly with an input of zero hours worked. A test coverage analyzer is used to produce a special instrumented version of PAYROLL which can count the number of times each logic segment is executed. Then all of PAYROLL's test cases are run. The results show that the logic path for zero hours has not been executed.

The maintenance world, we have already stated, is a microcosm of the software development world. All the tasks of the developer become tasks of the maintainer. Software verification practices are no exception. The software maintainer has a strong requirement to maintain a reliable product.

A large quantity of tools and techniques has become available to the software verifier in recent years. A comprehensive list is defined and discussed in a companion to Software Maintenance Guidebook, and the reader is referred to *Software Reliability Guidebook,* Prentice-Hall, 1979, Glass, for a complete discussion of verification aids. No attempt to replicate that information will be made here.

Other recent sources of verification-related information are refs. [6, 10, 12, 19, 20, 26, 29, 30–33, 37, 38, and 53].

Version Control

INPUT	PROCESSING	OUTPUT
1. The modules that make up a system.	1. Select those modules that make a particular version, and create it. 2. Track the relationships between modules—sibling modules, and derivation parents. 3. Control access to system creation by authorization passwords.	1. A version of the system consisting of a coordinated set of modules. 2. Printed list of inter-module relationships.

Example of Usage: The modules for the instrumented version of PAYROLL are different from the current production version of PAYROLL. That, in turn, is different from the previous version, which contained a now-obsolete FICA (social security) deduction calculation. Develop a system to ensure that no experimental or obsolete modules are used in constructing the current version.

The developer of a software system sees his final product as a gleaming software monolith of impeccable quality. The maintainer immersed in the realities of keeping that system functioning sees that product somewhat differently. A software system of any size and usefulness will actually exist as a series of versions. Versions come into being because no software system is ever change-free. Whether the changes are due to error correction or revised requirements, over a period of time there will be many versions of a software product.

The problem is: How do we keep track of these versions? The problem is a complicated one, because each version is made up of a (probably large) number of modules, and each module may or may not be different from one version to the next. To make matters worse, each module exists in at least two forms—source and object—and it is even possible for an object module to change when the source does not (e.g., when a global data base or external reference or copy file changes).

Automated tools have only begun to approach this problem. Manual tracking via a discipline called "configuration management" (see section 4.2.4) is still the state of the art. But an automated configuration management system, sometimes called a *version control* system, is beginning to appear [7].

Version control must track things at two levels: (1) at the module level, which modules are associated with each other (e.g., source and object) and how modules are derived, and (2) at the system level, which modules should be collected and linked to form a specific version.

The problem of version control is a specific application of a more general data-base problem. A module must be linked both to its associates or "siblings" (variant forms of the module) and to its derivation parent (the module and tool from which it was created). A system must be linked to its constituent modules bidirectionally, so that it is clear what the system consists of and which systems a module is part of.

A version control system may also need a system protection mechanism. Usually, for a large software system, changes may be made only under certain circumstances (e.g., approval from a change board). Thus, there must be capability both for relatively uncontrolled experimental version construction (for test purposes), and tightly controlled version construction for production systems. This suggests some solutions out of the computer security discipline, such as passwords and locking mechanisms.

The problem is complicated if there are several maintainers simultaneously working on a system. Can they both experimentally update the same module at the same time? Create overlapping experimental versions at the same time? If they are to be kept separate, how can they be kept separate?

The tasks to be solved by a version control tool are clear. The complexity and variety of those tasks, however, have kept the number of truly generic solutions to a minimum. Here, as in other software maintenance areas, some advanced development and experimental implementation approaches are needed to define the best solution methodologies.

The Supercompiler

INPUT	PROCESSING	OUTPUT
1. Total software system.	1. Compile and link the system. 2. Analyze cross-system communication. 3. Support system symbolic debug. 4. Optimize system for size and/or execution time.	1. Normal compiler and linker outputs in system-optimized form. 2. System communication information. 3. Symbolic debug facility for executing program. 4. Program instrumentation.

Example of Usage: The software for system ABRACADABRA, coded in Ada, is to be rebuilt. The supercompiler is used to produce the object code, complete with symbolic debug facilities for an interactive tester, and with test coverage analysis capability. A system-wide cross-reference list is produced at the same time.

Sprinkled throughout the previous sections of this book we have mentioned ideas for the improvement of the tools available to the maintainer. This section is an attempt to aggregate these tools into a unified system which the authors choose to call a *supercompiler.* Such a system does not exist yet, to the best of our knowledge. Parts of it exist, usually as semicompatible but distinct tools; but some parts do not yet exist at all. In the world of the future, when maintenance assumes its rightful place in the focus of computing attention, the supercompiler may in fact become a reality.

In order to understand the supercompiler concept, we must first define a "machine" upon which the supercompiler exists. It consists of a computer and a set of run-time routines called collectively "the operating system." The operating system is the *minimal* set of routines needed to connect the physical resources attached to the computer to the logical device or resources provided to the programs or tasks which operate on the computer. The supercompiler will then manage all of the programs within the software system. It "knows" every piece of the system. It has built-in knowledge of the entities that operate upon and are operated upon. That is, it maintains the source program modules, which are the human-readable representations of all functions; it "knows" the data base that is operated upon by these modules; it understands the relationship between source modules and their object modules, which are the "unsystemized" versions of the programs; and it manages the collection of various pieces or programs into larger entities which we call "systemization." It also recognizes that different versions of the same source/object/descriptor modules are possible and allows the substitution of these elements for each other. It is responsible for the execution of a module, at least to the extent that when the module "errs" or aborts, it is able to report the "system state" or module state in terms that are related to the symbolic (human-readable) source program. Failures are reported in terms of the variables referenced by the module and the subprograms it has invoked. It does not report the address at which the operating program blew up. It reports that program XYZ failed when executing statement number 27 in procedure ABRACADABRA because variable ABC was used as a subscript and ABC had a value of 19, too large to subscript array SMALL_ARRAY.

Additionally, since the supercompiler "knows" all the parts of the system, it can report all the modules that reference a piece of data, what values it is set to, what uses of that variable are made, and so on. This concept, as we said, ties together some specific ideas mentioned earlier in this guidebook, such as the procedure-oriented and data structure cross-reference listings of the system cross-reference lister, the debug concepts, the more sophisticated text-editing concepts, the reformatter, all of which are touched upon in section 3.2.1.1, and it can in fact include many of the verification aids also mentioned by reference in section 3.2.1.1. The compiler, because of the data it collects in the process of analyzing the programs that make up a software system, is capable of doing much more than we have come to expect of it.

The supercompiler should have at least the following capabilities:

1. Ability to integrate compilations for a large number of programs. The data that are global to all programs can then be analyzed for system impact.

2. Recreate a program's (or system's) entire environment sym-

bolically (at the HOL level) using a dump (snapshot) and descriptive modules.

3. Optimize not only individual programs, but a whole system.
4. Produce a system cross-reference list.
5. Produce a matrix or tree structure or network showing total system structure.

How the supercompiler could function. The structure of production-quality compilers is, by now, fairly predictable. There is an operating system interface, which centralizes all the service requests the compiler makes on the executive, and handles the overlay structure of the compiler, if any. In successive phases—often overlaid over one another—the following functions are performed:

1. Source processing—the source language is read and parsed, creating a symbol table in which all name-relevant information is saved, and an intermediate language file in which all the actions of the program are concisely expressed.
2. Optimization—the intermediate language is massaged to eliminate redundant actions, producing a newer and more streamlined and optimized intermediate language.
3. Code generation—the revised intermediate language is processed into object code for a particular computer, with such local optimizations as register allocation performed.

Until now, the output of a compiler has been this optimized object code, supported of course by appropriate listings and diagnostics. It is becoming apparent that the compiler is capable of producing additional outputs of considerable value.

We have already mentioned various kinds of cross-reference listings. The procedure-oriented and data reference cross-reference listings could be created without requiring any change in the traditional compiler structure mentioned above—the source processor already has available sufficient information to play that role. The system cross-reference lister, however, requires a break with tradition—the compiler must save the symbol tables of the constituent programs of a system in order to analyze all of them together once the whole system has been compiled.

However, saving symbol tables has other merit. If source-level debug is to become a reality, the symbol table must be available at program execute time so that the debug portion of the supercompiler can have the symbolic information it needs to report problems back to the programmer. Thus, we have now identified two reasons for making the compiler symbol table a standard compiler output.

In fact, the supercompiler will produce this kind of output, and more, in an entity we will generically call the *descriptor module.* The descriptor module will be responsible for containing supporting (descriptive) information needed by any follow-on supercompiler phases. As another example, via the descriptor table a data-base initialization program could easily be constructed which would contain sufficient information to validity check and consistency check the presetting of a massive data base (a requirement for this kind of program is frequently contained in real-time systems, where it may be desirable to modify the system data-base values without recompiling the whole system).

Another class of maintenance tools whose services could easily be provided by the supercompiler are those which "instrument" a program for some reason. *Instrumentation* is the process of spontaneously generating extra code so that the program can perform some measuring function while it executes. For example, a "test coverage analyzer" adds instrumentation so that a program may count the number of times each segment of its logical structure is executed; or an "assertion checker" adds instrumentation code so that programmer-specified assertions may be checked and diagnosed during execution. These kinds of functions are almost trivial additions to the traditional compiler, and therefore are obvious candidates for supercompiler capability.

Still another class of tools implementable within the supercompiler framework is the so-called *preprocessor.* Whereas the tools mentioned earlier function during and/or after the traditional compiler phases, the preprocessor operates before it, translating some other language into that processed by the source processor. For example, a "very high order language," one specific to a narrow application domain; or a "structured language," a constrained version of the base language; or a "shorthand language," a simplified version of the base language—any of these could be translated into the base language by the preprocessor portion of the supercompiler. (Perhaps the base language could have a macro-like facility to generalize the preprocessor function.)

Once the mental barrier that restricts the compiler to its traditional roles has been passed, it is to be expected that other and more exciting concepts can be provided by the supercompiler. Probably the best summary of these concepts to date is provided in ref. [51]; and in fact it would not be surprising to see the first supercompiler come into existence to support the new Department of Defense Ada programming language (ref. [60]).

An interesting parallel to this discussion of the supercompiler may be found in ref. [58], which discusses what might be called a "superlanguage."

The supercompiler—problems. It has already been mentioned that the supercompiler is beyond the state of the software art as we currently practice it. Partly, this is simply because no one has tried in the past to tie these fairly diverse functions together. That particular problem can be overcome by some earnest implementer deciding to design and build a supercompiler. However, there are some other problems. They are best illustrated by telling a story.

Over 20 years ago the first step toward a limited-scope supercompiler was taken. The Universal Computer-Oriented Language, UNCOL [48], was defined to facilitate the construction of a family of compiler source processors that could communicate with a family of code generators via UNCOL, a common intermediate language. By means of this scheme, any language for which a source processor was created could generate code for all the computers for which a code generator had already been written. The idea was brilliant—but it has continued to resist successful implementation. In recent years, the Air Force's JOCIT (Jovial Compiler Implementation Tool), the University of California at San Diego Pascal PCODE implementations, the UNIX-based C compiler, and probably some others, have come close. The problem is that we just don't know enough about intermediate languages to define one that is independent of all source languages and code generations and susceptible to high-quality optimization.

The same problem plagues the supercompiler. In spite of the academic attention focused on compiler work, there are still some significant unanswered questions in the intermediate language area. Further focused research is needed here. Additionally, some standards activity would be helpful. At least the symbol table, part of the descriptor module output, could have a standardized external representation (allowing the internal representation to be compiler specific). Then a common system cross-reference lister and/or debug package would support a family of supercompilers for a variety of language—or, in fact, the supercompiler itself could support more than one language.

There in the future, then, lies the supercompiler. Some of it is achievable with state-of-the-art knowledge and compiler structure. Some of it calls for knowledge and standards advances. But all of it—when it comes—will be of value to the software maintainer, who is long overdue for the help a sophisticated support environment of this kind can give.

The section that follows describes another approach to the supercompiler. In this approach, a powerful set of separate tools is aggregated into an "environment." The environment can, with appropriate attention to the separate tools and their interfaces, perform the role of the supercompiler. Such systems, as we shall see, are currently in existence—although with more limited power than the concepts in this section.

INPUT	PROCESSING	OUTPUT
1. All materials a programmer needs to build a system.	1. All capabilities needed by a programmer: a. Document production facilities. b. Program text manipulation facilities. c. Test result analysis facilities. d. Configuration management facilities.	1. Tested software system ready for delivery.

Example of Usage: The programmer for PAYROLL wants to produce a (hopefully) final version of the program, correcting all known errors and with all documentation up to date. He invokes the Programmer's Workbench text editor, document generator, compiler, linker, test-case harness, and test-result analyzer facilities. Following successful testing, he sanctifies the new version by indicating to the configuration management program that it should replace the previous "best" version.

Programmer's Workbench

There is a growing belief that the software developer and maintainer needs special attention and special facilities—in short, a special environment—in which to do his job. Emerging from this belief has come a facility that has taken several forms, probably the best known of which is the Programmer's Workbench [21]. Close on its heels is the Ada Programming Support Environment (APSE) being developed by the Department of Defense [51]. In this concept, a computer is devoted to the task of supporting the developer/maintainer, and a special and relatively standardized set of tools is provided to assist him on that host computer.

Capabilities provided in such an environment might include the following:

1. Document production
2. Text editing of programs and test cases
3. Syntax checking of programs
4. Analysis and reduction of test results
5. Configuration management of programs and data bases
6. Management data processing

A more powerful environment might also provide

7. Compilation, linking, execution, and debugging of programs
8. Integration and regression testing of systems

Typically, this environment is supported on a "host" computer, which may or may not be the computer on which the system will eventually execute. This host is chosen for the friendliness of its environment to the developing/maintaining programmer. Given the predictability of the use of this host and its environment, the programmer may come to expect that software development, independent of the project for which the software is being developed, will be supported by a set of common and useful tools.

In the Programmer's Workbench concept, basic developmental work is done on a standard minicomputer (lashed to a larger host computer, where necessary, for such large-computer functions as compilation). This concept is especially useful at an installation where programmers develop systems for a variety of large computers, not all of which are user-friendly.

In the APSE concept, the entire environment is hosted on a large computer, including sophisticated compilation facilities. Code developed on the host may be executed on other "target" computers, frequently mini- or microcomputers dedicated to specific applications.

This "programmer's workbench" environment is obviously, then, a summing up of the content of the preceding sections. All the facilities needed by the programmer are wrapped together in one package. Although the package is designed primarily for the developer, it should have value to the maintainer as well.

3.2.1.2   TOOLS FOR ADMINISTRATION OF MAINTENANCE

One of the major requirements for maintaining a software system is another "system" (or set of tools) geared to handling the paperwork involved in the maintenance task. What we are proposing here is a full-blown, mechanized (read "computerized") management information system for software maintenance. Systems of this kind are beginning to be available in rudimentary form; parts of them have been discussed in the literature under the structured programming concept "Program Support Library" (PSL) [1, 29], and under the Programmer's Workbench concept.

From a change-control point of view, the capabilities of this system could include:

1. The ability to handle problem reports.
2. The ability to handle correction reports.
3. The ability to correlate problems and corrections and report exceptions.
4. The implementation of status reporting by selected criteria (e.g., anticipated completion date, type of change).
5. The implementation of release documentation.

Problem reports contain a wealth of data that a variety of people will find useful. Such information as problems listed by severity of impact on the user, or by anticipated closure date, or by effort required to fix, or by length of time open may be extracted from a data base of problem reports. The documentation aspects of problem reporting are discussed more fully in section 4.3. The maintainer's own need has been discussed in section 3.1.2. Suffice it to say, problem report generator types of tools are an essential component of the maintainer's management information system. For example, working from the file of problem reports and supplementary information, status reports might be prepared which would provide an up-to-date report on the current state of all problems.

Status reporting beyond the preceding discussion of change control demands a fairly well defined set of data which may be gathered and filed manually, but often is not gathered at all. Such facts should include:

1. Number of lines of code in the system.
2. Number of lines last reporting period.
3. Relationship between modified lines and specific changes.
4. Person assigned to each change.
5. Tasks assigned to each maintainer.
6. Total core used by the system.
7. Core utilization breakdown by module.

In addition to the others who need such reports—users and managers, for example—the maintainer himself needs to keep abreast of where he is and where he is going. "Has this problem been reported before? Have I already fixed this problem in a newer version? How are my modifications progressing?" These types of questions can be resolved more quickly if the maintainer uses automation methodology to support his own needs.

The area of a maintainer management information system is one needing further research and pragmatic exploration.

3.2.2   Techniques for Maintenance

Software maintenance is, unfortunately, a highly specialized work form which still has not leaped the barrier between science and art. As much as we try to formalize the scientific aspects of programming, we can still not evade the inherent nature of problem solving (i.e., the intuitive leap, the guess, the "art" of programming). This is particularly true when it comes to maintenance.

Until the day arrives when a scientific (or semiscientific) system of tools, such as those described in section 3.2.1, is available, the maintainer will be forced to live within his current imperfect environment. He will of necessity be forced to look at dumps, wander around unaided in the listing, try to correlate the design representation to the requirements and specifications, and so on.

Some of the available techniques to assist the maintainer in his job are given in the following section. Concepts of how to evaluate how maintainable a piece of software is are given in ref. [12].

3.2.2.1   PREVENTING MAINTENANCE

The best software maintenance is no maintenance at all. That is, no changes are needed because no errors were committed and all changes were anticipated. ("A stitch in time saves nine million," according to Heinlein.)

The second best software maintenance is maintenance made easy by carefully considered software development.

Both of these "bests" are so important that they should be repeated here (however, they are not, so please go back and read them again!).

The most important impact to be made on software maintenance is the mind-set which thinks "maintenance" while performing development. Each iteration of the design and implementation stage must have, as an inherent part of the process, the goal of making it easier for the "next guy." The next guy may be the designer working from the requirements, or the coder working from the design, or the tester working from the code and the specifications, or the maintainer—the ultimate "next guy"—who works with all of the above. And, of course, the "next guy" may be, and in fact quite often is, the same person as the current guy. The key question of the whole development process is: "How can I make the next guy's job easier?"

The answer to that question is at first thought simple. The primary management emphasis on software maintenance should be on pushing maintenance costs forward. Remember the pie chart in Chapter 1 (figure 1.1–1), which showed maintenance costs, both total and per error, to be overwhelmingly larger than the same costs in the other life-cycle phases? It may cost more to design and develop maintainable software, but the ultimate payoff—and it's a big one—comes later, when maintenance becomes inexpensive and responsive.

All of our discussion so far is as palatable as Motherhood. It is easy and popular to say: "Do the job right the first time." What is needed, however, are some explicit definitions and examples of what "doing it right" really is. The remainder of this section will deal in specifics.

Before moving on, however, there is one other matter to be dealt with. This section is called "Preventing Maintenance."* It is not called by the more popular phrase "Preventive Maintenance." The latter, in the world of software, is really a misnomer. Whereas in other fields there may be activities that can be performed after the product has been delivered to decrease its chances of failure, the analogy does not precisely work in software. Computer hardware, for example, is often tested periodically with a fixed set of tests to see if those functions which used to work still do. Software, however, does not break or wear out, and therefore the analogous activities are meaningless. If software contains an error, it has usually† been there since it was developed, and it will not spontaneously appear or disappear! "Preventing maintenance" is an up-front activity, performed before the software maintenance-life-cycle phase actually begins. "Preventive maintenance"— that which is done during maintenance to lessen the chance of failure— may also be somewhat appropriate in software, but it is discussed elsewhere in this book (e.g., regression testing, enhancement maintenance) and it is not referred to by that largely inappropriate title.

With that "up-front" explanation out of the way, let us move on to some specifics of "preventing maintenance." The sections that follow will describe a set of techniques that can be used to make the job easier for that ultimate "next guy," the software maintainer.

Modularity

The most important consideration by far in preventing maintenance is the use of modular code. Unfortunately, that's a fairly ho-hum statement. Everyone believes it. Everyone, in fact, thinks they write

---

*When dealt with as an element of software quality, this concept is often called "maintainability." A good functional breakdown of this trait is found in ref. [4].
†An exception is that of errors introduced with new changes.

modular code. The crux of the problem of modularity, however, is that some people's modular code is a lot better than other people's modular code. We all acknowledge the value of modularity, and we all believe we're doing it. The problem is: What, really, is it?

It's not an easy question to answer. Sure, some excellent definitions have appeared in the literature [31, 39, 40]. The problem is that to translate these good words into a modular design for a particular application solution is subject to a lot of individual judgments, and those judgments will only be as good as the people making them. Reference [34] does a good job of putting those judgments into an objective framework.

This section, while making its own verbal attempt to discuss what good modularity is, how to create it, and how to recognize it, will in the end rely heavily on the use of examples. There is a kind of "gut-feeling" aspect to good modularity which no amount of philosophy or directives can fully replace.

First, though, let's take a cut at a definition. Modular programming is the practice of implementing software in small, functionally oriented pieces. These pieces are called modules and are usually implemented as subroutines or functions or clusters of functions. (In some languages, "sections" or "procedures" may be used.) Each module is devoted to one or more tasks related to a function; the module may be accessed from one or several places in a software system.

(The preceding paragraph of text is itself an example of the use of modularity. It is taken intact from another book [14]. It performs the single function of defining modularity, and as such it is a module of information that might be invoked in several different books. Its usefulness as a module comes about because it attempts to address a limited subject area in a generic way. Had it contained material relevant to its environment in the other book, for instance, it would not have been useful here.)

Contemporary circumstances suggest a somewhat negative discussion of modularity, as well. There is a trend, part of the broader trend toward "structured programming," toward defining modules in terms of the number of lines of code they contain. Programming standards frequently contain a constraint of the form: "Programming modules shall contain less than X lines of code," where X is most frequently in the 50 to 100 range. It is the opinion of the authors that this is unfortunate. It is unfortunate because it focuses attention on the size aspect of a module rather than on its functional aspects. Granted, many good modules are small. But many other good modules are not small. Granted, small modules tend to be easy to understand. But a straightforward large module may also be easy to understand, and a complex small one difficult. The key criterion here is a crisp functional breakdown, not size.

The advantages accrued during maintenance from good modularity are many. If the function performed by a module must change, only that module need change; the impact does not ripple through the whole program. If a new need for a function arises, the existing module can be invoked at the point of need, with minor overall impact to the rest of the program. (In fact, a revision to a well-modularized program will often consist of a series of calls to already existing modules.) And if an error is found, the odds are that its correction will be restricted to one (or at most a few) modules. Further, once a module is tested and used in a program, it can reliably be used elsewhere in the program. Thus, changes are not only more reasonable in cost, but more reliable in execution.

Probably the best example of modularity in practice is the subroutine library concept. Each subroutine in the library performs a well-defined task or a set of well-defined tasks. Programmers need not code their own square root or sort function; the problem has been solved, and the result made available as a canned, tested, and ready-to-use package of code. It is the nearest thing to the plug-compatible concept that software offers.

But modularity is much more than an available library. Modules are the building blocks of software. The function identified need not be one with generalized, earthshaking repercussions. It may simply be one needed a half-dozen places in a particular program. Its existence may well make the difference between an easy-to-maintain program and one so unyielding to change that it eventually gets scrapped. For example, good modular programming usually dictates that external interfaces, such as input/output, be isolated into separate modules. Failure to do so can be at the very least extremely painful to the maintainer who receives an interface change.

Modules may take many forms. Most commonly, an external (or "separately compiled") subprogram is considered to be a module. In Algol-type languages, an internal procedure (defined within a larger program) may also be a module. In COBOL and some other languages, a section or other separable segment of code may be a module. And in its most modern form, a data base with its cluster of data-base manipulating processes may be a module. Again, the essence of the module is its separateness of function.

Data communication to a module is important. The generally preferred form of communication is via a parameter list, where only local data and formal parameters are known to the module. This method of communication is preferred because all data used by the module are identified and isolated; it is not possible for the module to have a surprising side effect on the code which invokes it, such as would happen if the module modified a global variable whose value was important to the environment where the invocation of the module occurred.

However, the ideal of full use of a parameter list is not always attainable. The module may need to access a larger quantity of data than is convenient to specify in a parameter list at each point of call, for instance. In those circumstances, the data communication may be via global data, such as common or compool data. (Common is used in Fortran, and compool in JOVIAL and its derivatives, to centralize the declaration of data needed throughout the component modules that make up a program. The common/compool block itself becomes a separate module, or more than one separate module, of the program.)

Acknowledging this need, modern programming languages frequently include the "cluster" concept. A data base and its family of manipulating procedures is isolated from the rest of the program. A program needing some or all of the cluster must explicitly import it. The cluster itself can distinguish between data and procedures that may be exported and those that may not. Thus the side-effects problem is at least isolated and bounded [41, 42].

Modules that communicate data only by parameter lists are said to be "completely closed." Note that a completely closed module may easily be transported to another program or project, much like a library routine. Modules that also access global data are said to be "partially closed." Note that a partially closed module in effect has entwined data roots which link it to its program and make it much harder to transport. Note further that the cluster, which explicitly identifies its exports and carries its necessary data base with it, is essentially a closed module.

But enough of verbiage about modularity. It is time for some looks at examples of good and bad modularity.

Modularity example. Suppose that you have been asked to define a file management system which will be used to support one or more file-access application systems. After an appropriate initial design period, you realize that the solution breaks down rather crisply into a number of user service functions. You must be able to

1. Create a file
2. Destroy a file
3. Write onto a file
4. Read from a file
5. Search in a file
6. Add to a file
7. Remove from a file

Underlying these functions will be a data base keeping track of file information.

To satisfy these requirements, you create a module that performs each of those tasks. CREATE, for example, will take as input the name of the file to be created, and return, having updated the data base to include the new file. SEARCH will take as input a file name and a key piece of information to be sought in the file, and will return with the file positioned to that information and/or the file location of that information.

Note that each module/function is a well-defined set of tasks, and will be a fairly simple piece of code. The elaborateness of the total problem has been nicely broken down into easily solvable individual problems.

An Ada programming language definition of these modules would look like this:

```
Procedure CREATE (FILE_NAME) is
begin
   --perform the data base tasks necessary to create a file
end CREATE;
```

```
function SEARCH (FILE_NAME;KEY_NAME) return
   FILE_INDEX is begin
   --perform the identification of the file and the search for the
   --given key
   --then obtain the file index of the sought file
end SEARCH;
```

As you write each function, you realize that the data base must be referenced by each function, and in fact that it need not and should not be referenced by any other function. You realize that what you have is a cluster situation; the data base and its manipulating routines form a separable grouping of information, with a unique and well-defined set of interactions.

The Ada language definition of the cluster (called a package module in Ada) would be something like this:

```
package FILE_MANAGER is
   --all user service interfaces are defined here
   procedure CREATE (FILE_NAME);
   --other file manager functions
   function SEARCH(FILE_NAME;KEY_NAME) return
      FILE_INDEX;
end FILE_MANAGER;
package body FILE_MANAGER is
   --Implementation of the user services is defined here
   --but the user cannot see how they are implemented
   --the data base is also declared here.
procedure CREATE (FILE_NAME) is
begin
   --same code as discussed before
end CREATE;
--similarly for all other implementations
function SEARCH (FILE_NAME;KEY_NAME) return
   FILE_INDEX is
begin
   --same code as discussed before
end SEARCH
end FILE_MANAGER;
```

Two things are especially worth mentioning here: (1) the Ada package or cluster is broken into two parts, its external interface and its implementation (this is a nice example of modularizing all by itself); and (2) modularity in this example has now become hierarchic, with some modules containing other modules. This is modularity at its best; each function is crisply distinguished from each other function; the modular interrelationships are well defined; and except for those interrelationships, the modules are totally isolated from each other.

You might wonder how this same problem could be badly modularized. Several disgusting possibilities might be considered:

1. The whole file management system could have been embedded in the application that needed it.
2. The data base could have been separated from the application, but the functions performed in-line there.
3. The functional service routines (create, search, etc.) could have been intertwined with one another rather than separated into different procedures.

The possibilities for badness are, in fact, endless!

Program Structure

Much has been said in very large print, over the last 10 years, about structured programming. It is ballyhooed by both the knowing and the not-so-knowing of computing as being the greatest thing since the digital computer. Well, it's not.

That shocking statement, of course, requires an explanation. Structured programming, first of all, is not a universally well defined concept. It is defined in many places, of course (e.g., [1, 29, 59]), but not always consistently. Still, its essence is fairly well understood. It is the practice of programming using a limited but sufficient set of control constructs—which will not be named here because the references so abound with them as to make it virtually impossible for a reader of this book not to have seen them before! A lot of peripheral considerations have been hung on the concept, such as the use of chief programmer teams and top-down design and a program support library. But at heart, structured programming is the practice of programming using those control constructs that you've already read about elsewhere.

So then, what's wrong with structured programming? Not much, really, except the ballyhoo. Too many people are trying to take too much advantage of the need of too many software managers to be told that magic solutions to software's problems are just around the (structured) corner. Structured programming is no such magic solution. It is, however, an evolutionary improvement in the software development process, and as such it is worthy of use. In the overall hierarchy of preventing maintenance, modularity must rank as the most important concept. But program structure is not too far behind.

For the purpose of this book, *program structure* is defined as being those attributes of a program that contribute to the readability of its form. Use of structured programming constructs, for example, makes for a more readable and more aesthetically satisfying sequence of code. Begin-end groupings also make it easier to follow and understand code. And a consistent indentation policy, visually displaying the hierarchic relationships of a program's form, is extremely helpful, especially in complex programs. Perhaps even more important to program structure from a maintenance point of view is a consistent commentary policy. Comments that introduce each new element of program modularity and/or structure add significantly to its readability and contribute as well to its form. More will be said about other values of commentary later.

The distinction made here between modularity and structure may be a little perplexing to the reader. Isn't modularization, for instance, an approach to structure? The answer, of course, is yes. The reason that the two subjects are treated separately is partly historic, partly emphasis, and partly necessary. It is historic in the sense that "modularity" existed as much as 10 years before the advent of "structured programming." It is emphasis because the advantages of modularity are so large as to make it important not to clutter the subject with the ambiguities of "structured programming." It is necessary because program structure is a relatively meaningless concept in some programming languages, such as plain vanilla assembly language (as opposed to assembler enhanced with a strong macro capability), while modularity is usable in all such domains. Thus, the line between modularity and structure may be a tenuous one to walk, but it is an important one. Note that good modules may or may not possess good program structure, and note also that bad modules may also possess good program structure. The two subjects *are* distinguishable.

Somewhere on the line between modularity and structure is the subject of intermodule interfaces. Complex interfaces lead to unreadability and unaesthetic form, so the subject is included here. Crisp interfaces are another element of program structure.

As with modularity, program structure is best illustrated by examples. In the code that follows, look toward the attributes of program structure—control constructs, begin-end groupings, indentation, commentary, and interfaces—to make judgments about the quality of the code.

Program structure example. In the example for modularity, we discussed a file management system. Let us elaborate on the SEARCH function to illustrate both an example of good program structure, and the interaction between structure and modularity.

The example that follows is, again, coded in the Ada language.

```
function SEARCH (FILE_NAME; KEY_TYPE) return
FILE_INDEX is
begin
    --look for the specified key record in the specified file, returning
    --the index of its position
        for I in FILE_INDEX'FIRST..FILE_INDEX'LAST loop
        --Search the whole data base, from first to last
            if FILE_MAP (I) / = NULL
            --check data base for null or a match
                and then FILE_MAP (I) = FILE_NAME
                and then FILE_KEY (I) = KEY_TYPE then
                return I;
            end if;
        end loop;
        raise BAD_FILE;
        --raise an exception if the desired record is not found
end SEARCH;
```

This example illustrates two control constructs—the loop (for . . . loop . . . end loop) and the conditional (if . . . and then . . . then . . . end if). It also shows several begin-end groupings (begin-end SEARCH, loop-end loop, and if-end if), four levels of indentation, and quite a bit of commentary. (Interfaces were illustrated previously in our discussion of modularity.)

Imagine, if you will, the readability of this code without the indentations and the commentary. And imagine further being responsible for maintaining that difficult-to-read code. The impact of bad program structure is bad, indeed.

Data Structure

The computing literature seldom treats data structure and program structure as being subject to trade studies. Yet it is true that for many programs, one good data structure declaration may take the place of 100 lines of imperative code. And more important, from a maintenance point of view, modifying one data structure may take the place of modifying 100 scattered lines of imperative code.

An example is in order. In some programming languages, there are at least two ways of working with a string of bits or characters. One way is to declare the string as part of a structure:

```
STRUCTURE DATA_STRUCTURE; BEGIN
    ITEM CHARACTER_STRING 5 CHARACTERS;
    ITEM OTHER_VARIABLE 32 BITS;
END STRUCTURE;
```

and then manipulate the string by name:

```
OTHER_STRING=CHARACTER_STRING;
```

Another way is to use a byte-manipulating function to access the desired string:

```
OTHER_STRING=BYTE (CHARACTER_STRING,5);
```

Now suppose that the character string is referenced 100 times in the code. What is the impact, from the maintainer's point of view, if the character string must be increased from five to nine characters in length? Obviously, in the first case there is only one easily identified line of code to change, whereas in the latter there are 100 less easily found lines. The impact of data structure on program maintenance may be major.

(The example given above was chosen advisedly. The ongoing controversy over the impact of increasing the U.S. Postal Service's ZIP code length was mentioned previously. Clearly, proper attention to data structure in the past could have minimized the trauma of such a change.)

The example illustrates one way in which data structure is both important by itself and has an impact on executable code. It is also a middle-ground example; COBOL and PL/I, for example, carry the data structure capability to its finest contemporary extreme by providing elaborate edit-oriented data structures for formatting report data for printout. (A simple imperative move, for example, may result in stripping off leading zeros, inserting a decimal point, adding check protect characters, and placement of a leading dollar-sign character, if the target of the move is so declared.) At the other extreme, contemporary Fortran and Basic offer no data structure capability beyond the array. (This is probably the most serious weakness of the Fortran language.)

The data structure versus program structure dichotomy, as we have already seen, takes many forms. It even impacts the area of software design. One emerging methodology, often called the Jackson method [22], stresses designing the program structure by first looking at the data structures. According to this approach, an algorithm structure is highly related to data structure, and programs that obey data structure design will have more maintainable program structure as well. Obviously, different application areas have different levels of need for data structure orientation. Equally obviously, however, application areas that have need of data structuring capability have *deep* need of it.

One of the most noticeable attributes of large systems is the algorithmic transformation of a single data structure into another data structure. This process sometimes results from what Jackson calls a "structure clash"; at other times it is the result of proliferation of unnecessary code, or lack of design. In some large systems that have undergone an evolutionary life, the data have been transformed a number of times, sometimes adding information, sometimes creating a slightly different structure, until the "final" one is created which suits the current need. In order to resolve or halt this growth in the program's size, it is necessary to really analyze the problem from a different viewpoint. The intermediate data structures must be designed with a view toward the ultimate use of the information. For those programs that have structured data, proper attention to those structures must rank extremely high in the preventing maintenance hierarchy.

It is also important to group data appropriately. Where a set of data declarations interrelate, either by function or content, they should be grouped together for ease of understanding and modification. For instance, named common in Fortran or labeled compools in JOVIAL are preferable to one giant common or compool block. If a change is needed, it can be isolated to only one block, and only those modules which use that block need be recompiled.

The concept of abstract data typing is also receiving increasing attention as a method of structuring data. In this concept, all data must be declared to be of a particular type; types are defined in the language, but these may be supplemented by programmer-defined types; and associated with a type is a set of legitimate values which objects of a type may assume and a set of operations that may be performed on that type.

This kind of typing has these advantages: (1) the properties of a type are defined centrally at the type declaration, and if they change, they need only be changed in one place; (2) only the abstract properties of a type need be known to reference data of that type, with implementation details "hidden" in the declaration; and (3) strong type matching may be enforced by the compiler, eliminating type mismatch errors as a reliability/maintainability issue.

Only the most modern languages provide the full abstract data-typing capability described here. Traditional Fortran, COBOL, and Algol, for example, do not support it; however, Ada and Pascal do. For those languages that do not support it, there is no effective way of providing the capability.

Finally, it is important to name data effectively. Meaningful names are preferable, certainly, to randomly chosen ones. What do you suppose EMPLOYEE_NAME contains? Or EMPNAM?

This recommendation is not without controversy, however. Contemporary software standards often contain a requirement to name data based on their structure rather than their content. For example, an item of data that is defined in module XYZ and part of table TAB might be called XYZ_TAB_1. Certainly, this type of naming convention tells the maintenance programmer some important things about where the data came from. The authors believe, however, that it is counterproductive to the readability of programs. Perhaps some sort

of compromise is possible; for example, EMPLOYEE_NAME_XYZ_
TAB, where both the meaning and the structure are incorporated. The
result, unfortunately, may be a name the programmer will elect not to
use because of muscle cramps in his writing arm. (A good text editor
can help with this problem—the programmer can code shorter names,
then make a longer name readability substitution with only one
command for each name.) Often, readable (long) names are used for
global data, and shorter names for less important, local data. Thus, the
issue of naming conventions is sometimes related to the issue of scope.
Data structure example. Suppose that as part of the file management
example you have previously seen, each of the files has its own peculiar
format. For all files, all the records are (perhaps) of the same size, but
each file's records are of a different format from any other file. As is
commonly true of records, that format is heterogeneous—that is, the
record is made up of a lot of different kinds of data. Some of it may be
character strings, some of it integers, and some of it even floating-point
data.

Representing this sort of heterogeneous structure is easy in some
languages, and impossible in others. The Ada data structure is
illustrated below. Note that the structure is defined as an Ada TYPE;
that type may then be used within the language to create several
instances of that structure.

```
type RECORD_FORMAT_1 is
   record
      EMPLOYEE_NAME: array (1..30) of CHARACTER;
      EMPLOYEE_RATE: float;
      EMPLOYEE_HOURS: integer range 0..99;
   end record;
FILE1-RECORD: RECORD_FORMAT_1;
```

The record format for file 1 is thus defined to be of the type re-
cord_format_1; and it, in turn, consists of a 30-character string, a
floating-point number, and a two-digit integer. Note that each name is
chosen to clearly explain its content (in fact, this is enhanced by the
Ada language because even the type has a descriptive name of the data
itself).

The notion of grouping of data can perhaps best be illustrated by
the cluster concept, mentioned earlier in another context. Suppose that

associated with the file manager program is a file description table, a current file index, and a table relating files to physical locations. Obviously, this and all other pieces of file data-base information should be grouped together, since they are highly interrelated. If any of the data changes during system maintenance, all the data should be reviewed for impact; and more important, no other data (hopefully) would be impacted by the change.

This file management data base could be clustered with the access functions discussed earlier (e.g., create and search) to form a complete description of the file manager's content and function.

An Ada language description of this data cluster would be

```
package FILE_MANAGER is
   --all user services are defined here, as before
end FILE_MANAGER;
package body FILE_MANAGER is
   type FILE_DESCRIPTION_TABLE_FORMAT is
      record
         FILE_NAME: array (1..10) of CHARACTER;
         FILE_KIND: integer range 0..4;
      end record;
   type FILE_LOCATION is
      record
         FILE_NAME: array (1..10) of CHARACTER;
         FILE_POINTER: integer range 0. .32767;
      end record;
   FILE_TABLE: FILE_DESCRIPTION_TABLE_FORMAT;
   FILE_INDEX: integer range 0. .NUMBER_OF_FILES;
   FILE_LOC: FILE_LOCATION;
   --implementation of user services follows, as before
end FILE_MANAGER:
```

Now the data structure is grouped with the other code that requires it.

High-Order Language

It has almost become a given in discussions of software to cite high-order language as an underlying solution to most problems of the discipline. Software maintenance—including preventing maintenance —is no exception.

As with program structure, the subject is so well covered in the literature as not to need a fresh (or stale!) justification [25,59]. To help put the subject in perspective, however, it is interesting to note how many of the other preventing maintenance techniques are assisted by the use of an HOL.

Data structure, as described in the previous section, is largely impossible without the help of a good HOL (the use of arrays to simulate tree structures, and attempts to pack data without declarative packing, are extremely painful). Program structure is not quite so impossible, but still clumsy at best, in an assembler language—even one with capable macros. Modularity, however, is just as possible in assembler code as in an HOL. Of the preventing maintenance subjects to follow, most are HOL-independent. Documentation, however, is assisted in a major way by the improved readability of HOL.

It should also be noted that not all HOLs are alike. Pre-1977 Fortran, the second most popular language of all time (COBOL is number one) when measured by the number of users, is a very bad HOL for preventing maintenance. It offers modularity, to be sure, but it has limited or no capability for program structure, data structure, or parameterization (to be discussed in the next section). Algol-derivative languages correct most or all of these flaws. COBOL, for all the goodness of its data structures, is poor on modularity and program structure. The fact that these two languages survive as the leading languages of our time is strong evidence that maintenance considerations have played little part in language decisions in the past.

Examples of HOL code may best be seen by referencing the language reference manual for the programming language of your choice. Examples of particularly good HOL code may best be found in refs. [24 and 27].

Parameterization

Small things sometimes have great impact. *Parameterization* is one of those. The concept is simple enough. If a constant is used to represent the same entity in several places in a program and it could possibly ever change, give it a name and use that name wherever it is referenced. The importance of this technique comes if the constant is indeed changed. Then only the definition of the name must be changed, not the references. (Note the conceptual similarity of this technique to that of data structures. In fact, it can be stated generically that any technique that allows centralizing variable entities into a declaration is a good technique for preventing maintenance.)

Not all languages are equally helpful in providing this capability. Ironically, it is available more often in assembler language than in HOL. The macro facility, or an "equals" or "synonymous" mechanism (e.g., ARRAY_SIZE EQU 10) is almost always provided in assembler language. Rare, however, has been the HOL that supports it. The Air Force language JOVIAL offers the DEFINE, a limited macro capability: DEFINE ARRAY'SIZE "10". Again, advancing technology has ignored the needs of software maintenance.

It is not enough that the language support dynamic constants (those that may be initialized in some way, such as by a preset mechanism or an assignment statement). The value of parameterization is not fulfilled unless the value of the named constant is known and used at compile time. Note that a dynamic constant may not be used in a declarative statement, whereas a parameter may [e.g., DECLARE TABLE (TABLE'SIZE)].

An example of parameterization follows.

Parameterization example. A fundamental problem in computer applications is the detection of situations where a program's capacity is exceeded. All too often, the solution is no solution at all—the problem is simply ignored (and the program aborts ungracefully and mysteriously when the capacity is eventually exceeded).

More frequent, fortunately, is the situation where the program itself checks dynamically for the anomalous behavior. Upon detection of potential capacity overflow, it prints a warning message and performs some sort of recovery (perhaps either gracefully terminating, or resetting the data area pointer to a possibly safer non-capacity-overflow value).

The question is: What is the best way, from a maintenance point of view, to make such a test? The answer, as you might suspect, is related to parameterization.

Consider this example, coded in the Ada language:

```
FILE_TABLE_SIZE: constant integer: = 15;
FILE_TABLE: array (1..FILE_TABLE_SIZE) of FILE_LOCATION;
--assume that FILE_LOCATION is a record type, as defined before
```

```
function ADD (FILE_NAME) return FILE_INDEX is
begin
   --add a file to the file table
   for I in 1..FILE_TABLE_SIZE loop
     if FILE_TABLE(I)=FILE_NAME then return I; end if;
     if FILE_TABLE(I)=NULL then
       FILE_TABLE(I):=FILE_NAME; return I; end if;
   end loop;
   raise TABLE_OVERFLOW;
end ADD;
```

There are two places, entirely different in nature, where the capacity of the file table is expressed in the example—in the declared size of the table; and in the for loop, where it controls the number of times the loop is executed. If it becomes necessary to change the size of the table—to enlarge it, for example, after a spate of dynamically detected table overflows—then that change need only be made where the parameter itself is declared. The declaration of the table and the test loop do not care what the size of the table is; they only know that it has one, and that it is named.

This problem arises almost as frequently as there are data aggregates in a program. The declaration of such an aggregate should automatically be accompanied by a decision on whether the aggregate could ever overflow. If the answer is yes, use of parameterization is in order.

Data Communication

There are commonly three flavors of intraprogram data communication available to the programmer. (*Data communication* is defined here to mean the passage of data among modules.) One method is the use of parameter lists. Another is the use of global or common data. A third is the newly emerging concept of a cluster, where a constrained "semiglobal" data base is shared among a limited number of processes [41, 42].

Interprogram data communication is also important. Most commonly, this is provided by either passing data flags and blocks through an operating-system-provided communication area, or passing larger volumes of information on files. The UNIX concept of "pipes," in which predefined files are automatically passed from one program to the next, is a particularly elegant but sometimes overly simplistic solution to this problem [45].

Data communication was discussed previously under "modularity." It is brought up again here simply to highlight it as an important consideration in its own right in preventing maintenance. As stated previously, parameter passing is the preferred intraprogram data communication methodology from a purist point of view; reality, especially in large projects, frequently demands the use of global/common; and the cluster appears to be a valid way of bounding the hazards of unconstrained global usage. No analogous value judgments are made about interprogram communication.

An example of data communication follows.

Data communication example. Recall that procedures CREATE and SEARCH required certain parameters in order to perform their function properly—CREATE must be told the name of the file to be created, and SEARCH must be told both the file name and the name of a key to be looked up in the file. This information was passed to these procedures in the preferred data communication manner—as parameters. We had, for example, the calls

```
CREATE(FILE1);
SEARCH(FILE1,KEY1);
```

which request specific services for FILE1 and KEY1.

If there were only one file in the system—an unlikely event, as the problem has previously been stated, but still possible—then there would be no need to name it in a parameter list. If, further, there were a global variable named KEY1, which could be set by the user of CREATE and SEARCH and accessed by those routines, we might have

```
CREATE;
KEY1: = SOMETHING;
SEARCH;
```

The code is now certainly more terse, but less descriptive. More important, the possibility is left open that KEY1 may be accessed or set by other parts of the program. For example, suppose that the programmer is going to rely on the value of KEY1 set earlier:

```
CREATE;
KEY1: = SOMETHING;
...
SEARCH;
```

If the innocuous part of the program designated by ". . ." contains an assignment to KEY1, either in its initial coding or in subsequent modification, the SEARCH will be erroneous. It is this kind of problem that causes the use of global data to be considered undesirable.

Finally, suppose that file name and key name are not to be passed as parameters but are to be protected from erroneous stores (this kind of erroneous store is commonly called "clobbering"!). The concept of the cluster provides this capability:

```
package FILE_MANAGER is
    --user services are defined here
    --KEY1 is not defined here, and thus is not accessible from the
      outside
end FILE_MANAGER;

package body FILE_MANAGER is
    KEY1: integer;
    ...
    --implementation of user services is defined here
    ...
    KEY1: = SOMETHING;
    ...
    SEARCH;
    ...
end FILE_MANAGER;
```

The likelihood of KEY1 being clobbered between its assignment and the SEARCH call is now considerably lessened, since nothing outside the cluster can access it. This cluster provides the capability of global data, but with protection.

Defensive Programming

Murphy's Law (if anything can go wrong, it will) should be etched in big letters on the desk of every programmer. Given that the programmer's job is telling a big dumb machine (or, perhaps, in the modern world, a little dumb machine!) how to do things in excruciating detail leaves magnificent opportunities for things to go wrong.

Have you ever given anyone directions on how to get some place? Have you ever given a blind person directions on how to get some place? Think about the difference for a minute. The level of detail needed by the blind person only begins to approach the level of detail needed by a computer.

The wise programmer acknowledges that he will make mistakes, some of which will not show up in a program for years. He writes his program so that it has a good chance of self-detecting problems before they get out of hand, and pinpointing them so that the maintainer can quickly fix them. This thoughtfulness is another form of preventing maintenance. It is called here by the generic handle *defensive programming,* analogous to "defensive driving," the act of driving with the senses tuned to potential problems.

Defensive programming is a broad concept, and in some ways it is even application-dependent. However, some general principles may be applied. One general technique for defensive programming is that of *assertions* [53]. The program should contain whatever statements the programmer can make about acceptable program or data behavior, and furthermore it should have the capability to test those assertions to see if they are holding true. There should also be an exception mechanism which prints a diagnostic message identifying the violated assertion and the point of violation, and a recovery process for continuing or aborting after the diagnostic is produced.

The use of the word "assertion" may be misleading here. The term arose in the software world in connection with proof-of-correctness technology. That is not the context implied here. What we are talking about here is an extension of the already well known concepts of data editing and exception processing.

Assertions could be used, for example, to detect the following:

1.   Erroneous or improbable input data
2.   Erroneous or improbable output data

3. Erroneous or improbable data in general
4. Improper logic flow
5. Undesired procedure call side effects
6. Subscripts out of range
7. Uninitialized variable usage
8. Data storage overflow
9. Exception condition
10. Any other condition the programmer knows to be a fault

Some of these categories are worth spending a little more time on. Input data verification is a major category all its own. Tight testing of the validity of input data, especially if the input comes in from unskilled people, may be essential to the stability of a program (and the programmer!). Many a program "bug" has turned out to be undetected unadulterated garbage input. The result may be painful garbage output unless the problem is detected early.

Data storage overflow is another problem with serious repercussions. (This was mentioned earlier under "parameterization.") The programmer who cries "How was I to know the users would try to put 101 gizmos into an array of size 100?" is guilty of poor defensive programming. The proper approach is a simple assertion, at each point at which a value is stored in the array (or at the points where the subscript is incremented, if it is sequential), which detects the overflow, diagnoses it externally for the benefit of the user, and takes whatever recovery action is possible. Program behavior where this is not done is sometimes astoundingly abominable! (The authors wrote a program once that caused an undetected overflow of a compiler's symbol table. The compiler, having clobbered some adjacent unrelated memory, printed 512 meaningless error messages and then aborted!)

There is a difficult question about how many of these assertions should remain active in a program during its production usage, given that there is a size and time impact caused by the code needed to perform the assertion check. Some people say that they can't afford to leave assertions in a production program. Some others say they can't afford not to. The decision as to whether to, and how many to, probably has to be situation-specific. A cost/benefit study on specific assertions should be made, with some of them (the important and/or cheap ones) left in, and the others used only when conditions warrant.

There are techniques, however, to make it easy to leave in or remove the assertions. Some language processors can recognize assertions—they must be specified by a predefined syntax—and provide the option to ignore them or process them at compile time. Other language processors provide a "conditional compilation" facility, by means of which programmer-identified code of all kinds (including assertions) can be ignored or processed optionally. Obviously, some such facility is essential to the convenient use of assertions if the intent is to run with them in the program only part of the time (such as during a debugging run).

In addition to the assertion technique of defensive programming, there is the technique of *margins*. Some portion of the resources available to a system should be deliberately held back and not used by the current system. The reason for this, of course, is to leave room for the maintainer to do his job properly. Whether it is core memory or disk storage, if 100% of it is used by the original developer, the maintainer will find it extremely difficult or impossible to add new capabilities or correct old ones. Whether it is nanoseconds of I/O time or seconds of user response time, if all that are available have been consumed in the original solution, the maintainer is in trouble. In the early days of computing—and in today's microprocessors—it was (is) not unusual to spend half of the maintainer's time shrinking the program's resource requirements, and the other half adding new facilities and using up the resources so freed. This doubling of the already high cost of maintenance is usually intolerable by today's standards. Margins provide an escape valve for the inevitably harrassed maintainer.

Still another technique for the defensive programmer is the software cockpit recorder. This is a concept stolen from the world of airplane manufacturers, and means simply this—the software, as it executes, has the capability of leaving behind an audit trail recording significant events that occurred during program execution (e.g., modules entered, significant data variables set to significant values, iterations converged, phases completed, assertions recorded, etc.). By means of the content of the cockpit recorder, if the software crashes, it may be possible to reconstruct why it crashed (the analogy to aircraft crashes is obvious). Note that this concept could equally well have been stolen from the world of the C.P.A., as the subtitle "audit trail" so clearly points out!

The granularity of the audit trail may be maintained as a conditional compilation option in the source code. For example, the normal software production run might record only the entry into major system phases, for efficiency reasons; but for postmortem analysis of a crash, it would be possible to recompile with a considerably increased granularity (to trace module entries and key data variables, for example). If optimization considerations permit, these granularity controls could even become an execute-time option, removing the need for recompilation prior to a crash-analysis rerun. (It is interesting to note that in the software world, the luxury of recreating the crash with an improved cockpit recording is an option!)

Yet another defensive programming technique is the *flagging and aggregating of unsafe programming practices.* It is an embarrassment to the software world, but a truism nonetheless, that programmers sometimes engage in (gasp!) unsafe practices. The reasons vary from simple feasibility ("the language prevented me from solving my problem without a little cheating"), to optimization ("I couldn't meet my timing requirements without some tricky coding"). As these examples illustrate, contrary to sometimes-voiced opinion, unsafe practices are not merely an aberration performed by devious programmers, but a necessity performed at one time or another (hopefully, rarely) by all programmers.

In case this idea needs even more credibility, consider these examples of instances where unsafe programming is required in many programming languages:

Example	Unsafe Practice
Hash code algorithms	Type violation—a character string, for example, may have arithmetic performed on it.
Character set conversion	Type violation—a character may be used as an index to access an array of characters.
Sin/cos routine	Single entry to a subprogram—The sin and cos algorithms are typically coded as one routine with two entry points.
Exception resumption	GOTO use—returning to the code following the raising of a recoverable exception.
Memory dumping, garbage collection, etc.	Type violation—a location in memory may be treated as a bit string, for example, regardless of what its type really is.
Interrupt servicing, etc.	Absolute addressing—a particular piece of data may only be available at a specific memory address.

The proper approach to unsafe programming, then, is to (1) acknowledge that it is sometimes necessary, (2) design languages and standards to minimize the number of such occurrences by providing enough power for the programmer to do safely and clearly those things that must be done, and (3) make provision for a reporting mechanism so that those unsafe practices that remain are both annotated in the listing at the point of their occurrence (*what* is the unsafe practice? *why* was it used?), and summarized at the end of the program for manager/programmer review.

At present, this summary must be programmer-prepared. However, help is coming! The Ada language has an explicit Unsafe Conversion methodology, and Ada compilers can prepare the summary automatically.

The advantages to the software maintainer of being able to find and understand unsafe code segments is that their role in any fixes or revisions can be quickly determined.

Some examples of defensive programming follow.

Defensive Programming Examples

In the Ada language, some assertion capability is built into the language. For example, the programmer may specify the range of a variable at its point of declaration:

    ARRAY_SIZE: integer range 1..100;

Then if an assignment to the variable outside that range occurs, the compiler or the execution-time support routine is obligated to diagnose that occurrence or to raise an exception (optionally obligated, since there are times when the execution-time overhead of such checks is undesirable):

    ARRAY_SIZE: = –5; --a diagnostic should be given at compile time
    or
    I: = 100;
    ...
    ARRAY_SIZE: = I+1; --a range exception should be raised during
        execution.

Even without the range assertion, the programmer may provide the defensive check:

```
ARRAY_SIZE: = XX;
if ARRAY_SIZE < 1 or ARRAY_SIZE > 100 then
    PRODUCE_DIAGNOSTIC (ARRAY_SIZE);
    ABORT_GRACEFULLY;
end if;
```

In some implementations of assertions, the programmer makes an explicit range declaration and then is given a diagnostic if it is violated at execute time:

```
!RANGE_ARRAY_SIZE (1..10);
...
ARRAY_SIZE = 101; --a diagnostic will be given during execution.
```

As previously mentioned, range checking is certainly not the only possible kind of defensive programming, although it may well be the most important. Relationships between variables, or procedure call side effects, for example, are also important:

```
!RELATION FIRST_THINGEE < = NEW_THINGEE < =
    LAST_THINGEE AND NEW_THINGEE > 0;
```

is a relationship for which an assertion processor could detect violations and produce diagnostics; and

```
!CALL(FIRST_VARIABLE;SECOND_VARIABLE);
EXECUTE_PROCEDURE(PARAMETER);
```

is an assertion request to check for possible side effects of procedure EXECUTE_PROCEDURE on variables FIRST_VARIABLE and SECOND_VARIABLE. Note that in the absence of an assertion capability, the same checks could be coded less conveniently:

```
(a) if NEW_THINGEE < FIRST_THINGEE or
       NEW_THINGEE > LAST_THINGEE or
       NEW_THINGEE < = 0 then
```

```
      PRODUCE_DIAGNOSTIC(NEW_THINGEE);
   RECOVER; end if;
(b) SAVE_FIRST: = FIRST_VARIABLE:
      SAVE_SECOND: = SECOND_VARIABLE;
   EXECUTE_PROCEDURE(PARAMETER);
   if FIRST_VARIABLE/ = SAVE_FIRST or
      SECOND_VARIABLE/ = SAVE_SECOND then
      PRODUCE_DIAGNOSTIC(EXECUTE_PROCEDURE);
      RECOVER;
   end if;
```

Programming Standards

Programming standards are the requirements placed on a programmer by his environmental control structure. They may be dictated by his management, or by a contract, or perhaps by his peers. They are over and above, however, the requirements of his application or his language or his compiler. They are usually imposed for the expressed benefit of improving programming practices and increasing management control. The chief actual beneficiary, to the extent that there is one, is usually the maintenance programmer. Programs written to standards, whatever else may be said about them, are usually more predictable and therefore often easier to get aboard more quickly. That, in turn, contributes to preventing maintenance [57].

Programming standards may, however, be misused. All too often a set of programming standards is one programmer's (or manager's, or worst of all, nonprogrammer's) favorite bag of tricks. Sometimes, too, it is the reflection of the latest trends in software engineering technology, whether they are really understood or not. The result is often a mixture of proceduralized goodness and nonsense.

Probably what is really needed here is a set of standards for standards writers:

1. Don't specify unless you're sure you're improving things.
2. Make the specification lean, so that it can be remembered.
3. Don't redundantly standardize those things already required by the language or system.
4. Stress guidelines, not standards.
5. Stress content; specify form only when necessary.

6. Define the process for escape from the standards.
7. Think of the programmer as a practicing professional, not as an amateur.

With this undergirding, perhaps standards *can* become the help to the maintainer which they should be.

Typical contemporary standards include naming conventions (a set of rules for naming program data or logic entities), complexity limitations (a set of rules limiting such things as the number of lines of code per module), construct limitations (a set of rules bounding the allowable language forms, such as GOTOs or ALTERing GOTOs), and so on. As we have already seen, structured naming conventions and lines of code per module restrictions have some bad side effects. So, obviously, does control construct limitation, at least in contemporary languages.

Programming standards examples. One very large software project (part of a considerably larger space project) has developed a standards manual that is nearly 100 pages long! The standards that follow are some of the higher-quality excerpts from that manual.

1. Global data bases shall be partitioned into blocks that are organized to minimize the number of modules requiring access to the block.
2. Variables shall be assigned a single name (and not be EQUIVALENCEd or OVERLAYed).
3. Input/output requests shall be handled centrally by an executive module with submodules, one per external device.
4. The program design language shall be inserted in the progam resulting from that design, as comments.
5. A component development folder shall be developed and maintained for each computer program component. The content of the folder shall include
   a. A cover sheet
   b. A change log
   c. Component requirements
   d. Component design

   e. Current component listing
   f. Component test plan
   g. Component test results
   h. Problem reports
   i. Reviewer comments
   j. Design notes
6. Names shall be chosen to emphasize function but to also include program structure. Structure shall be shown by
   a. Making component name part of each name in the component, abbreviated as follows. . . .
   b. Making data aggregate or block name part of each name in the aggregate, abbreviated if necessary as follows. . . .
7. Structured coding constructs shall be emphasized.
8. Commentary shall be provided at least as follows:
   a. Detailing the function and interface of each subprogram
   b. Describing the use and content of each data variable
   c. Explaining each subfunction
   d. Explaining any tricky or complex code
9. Nesting depth shall be minimized.
10. Modules shall be determined by function, but kept to an average of 100 lines of code per module.

Documentation

Much of the preceding discussion of preventing maintenance has been on a "first things first" basis. Modularity is by far the most important preventing maintenance technique. Program and data structure are also important, but less so. Programming standards, for all the attention they get, contribute considerably less (except to the extent that they enforce the higher-ranked concepts).

Documentation has been saved for last, however, not because of its unimportance but because (1) it is somewhat different from all the others, and (2) it is discussed in considerable depth elsewhere in this book. The point will be made many times in this book that we have been proceeding all wrong in defining program documentation from the maintainer's point of view. The documentation, at least at the detail level, should be found as commentary in the program listing, not in a separate volume.

This section will not explore that reasoning further, but instead will make some explicit suggestions about what kind of commentary, and where, and how much, should make up this form of documentation. Before proceeding, it should be pointed out that *good documentation* (read "commentary") *is as essential as any other technique to preventing maintenance.*

Commentary should occur in *at least* the following places in a program:

1. At the beginning of each module, include the module name, the current date, the module's function, its inputs and outputs, its limitations and restrictions, including assumptions, its error processes, and the name of the developer. Major modules should also include the history of module modifications: for each change, the date, maintainer's name, purpose of the change, and its scope.

2. At each subfunction, whether it be a straight sequence of code or a logic branch or a begin-end block, an explanation of that subfunction.

3. At each interface, a clear definition of the interface and a reference for further information about the other side of the interface (where possible).

4. At each group of functionally or otherwise related declarations, an explanation of the role and makeup of the group.

5. At each declaration, an explanation of the role of the item and the meaning, if any, of its possible values.

6. At each difficult-to-understand program portion, an explanation of what the code does and why a complex solution was necessary.

The problem in commentary, however, is seldom in knowing what to do. It is doing it. Therefore, the preventing-maintenance-oriented manager or technologist must have a process for causing the proper commentary to be inserted and a process for auditing to be sure that it is. The peer code review [1, 29], which has many other benefits (and an associated high up-front cost!), is one good place to remind the programmer to provide adequate commentary, and in fact is probably the development milestone by which all commentary should be in place. (If the programmer has inserted the design language as commentary, there is probably not a whole lot of additional commentary to add.) The audit process should occur soon afterward. Alternatively, the language processor or an automated code auditor can check conformance to commentary and other standards relatively painlessly.

Good documentation, like good writing, is a specialized art. Some examples follow.

Documentation example. Our old friend the SEARCH function was discussed earlier, but mostly to illustrate some principles of program structure. Below we find another cut at SEARCH to illustrate good commentary practices from the point view of making a program more self-documenting:

```
--FUNCTION SEARCH
--INPUT = FILE_NAME AND KEY_TYPE,
--OUTPUT = FILE_INDEX
--searches the file directory for the given file, then
--searches the file for the given key, and
--returns a pointer to the file in FILE_INDEX
--raises BAD_FILE exception if the requested file is not in the
--directory, or
--raises BAD_KEY exception if the sought key is not in the file
--coded Dec. 25, 1981 by Studs Axeswinger
function SEARCH (FILE_NAME; KEY_TYPE)
   return FILE_INDEX is begin
--look for the given key record in the given file
   for FILE_POINTER in FILE_INDEX'FIRST..
      FILE_INDEX'LAST loop
   --first find the file
      if FILE_MAP (FILE_POINTER) = FILE_NAME
      then goto FIND_KEY;
      end if;
   end loop;
   raise BAD_FILE; return; --couldn't find file
```

```
≪FIND KEY≫ RECORD_COUNT : =0;--got the file
   while KEY_TYPE = FILE_KEY loop
      --then find the key
      READ (FILE_POINTER); --reads a record
      RECORD_COUNT := RECORD_COUNT + 1;
      --remember where you are
   end loop;
   FILE_INDEX := RECORD_COUNT; -- save output
   return;
begin--exception handling block
   exception
      when END_OF_FILE raise BAD_KEY; return;
      --couldn't find key
   end
end SEARCH;
```

3.2.2.2   HARD WORK AND PERSPIRATION

No matter how well the preventing maintenance task is performed, we must face the onerous fact that the majority of the effort in maintenance will be simply hard work. Only by thorough, painstaking attention to the detail of the program can some problems be resolved. In many cases, the solution is arrived at only by enumerating all the possible sources of error and eliminating them one by one until what remains, no matter how implausible, must be the solution. Very often, the mere listing of possible solutions will provide the necessary insight to bring this about. Some problems will require many iterations of the process, each iteration providing a further understanding of the entire design of the program. After several occurrences of this scheme, with the elapse of time inherent in the process, the solution may spring into mind, via the "intuitive leap" mentioned in an earlier section. But understand, the leap is not possible without the training and understanding provided by studying the problem thoroughly.

There exists a class of software problems which are characteristically the most difficult to solve. These problems almost invariably look like computer failures. The program fails to operate properly in some unique circumstance. Often, it is impossible (or at least difficult) to reproduce the problem. Sporadic problems of this kind require the ultimate in hard work and perspiration to correct (and a large dose of patience besides). All the techniques of normal problem correction must be employed, and in addition the temptation to hope the problem will go away if it is ignored must be fought off!

3.2.2.3   PRODUCT IMPROVEMENT

Improvements must *continually* be made in the quality of the program. Often these improvements take the form of injecting the preventing maintenance techniques that should have been included by the developer. Methods of making such improvements include:

1. Modularize: Where code is repeated, make it into a callable procedure. This will also tend to shorten the source code, often considerably. Further, it tends to isolate functional areas for ease of subsequent change.
2. Eliminate GOTOs and labels where they are not necessary: An unwholesome advocacy of GOTO elimination will lead to more problems than it solves, but in very obvious cases of nonserial code that should be serial, move it!
3. Make modules mutually suspicious: Let each module make consistency and appropriateness checks on questionable data from other modules. This will at least catch errors or deficiencies earlier than letting them slide through. Where variables are known to have a specific range of values, check for their being outside of bounds. This is the assertion-checking technique mentioned earlier in this section.

3.2.2.4   LARGE SYSTEMS—A METHOD
OF APPROACH

Large systems present a set of unique problems to both the software builder and the software maintainer. Although solutions to those problems are still being sought, the most common methodology used to structure these problems is the addition of formality—more formal specifications, more formal design representations, more formally defined system interfaces, more formally defined expected test outputs, and more formal test reporting.

This kind of formality may prove useful to the software maintainer. A particularly good discussion of the approach is found in ref. [18]; a trouble-plagued software maintenance effort is enhanced by a useful experiment in which the system is reconstructed in a more formal manner, especially using an up-to-date and maintained software requirements specification.

When a problem arises in a large system, there are also some special considerations to be made.

The method of approach to problems in large systems probably should include the following steps:

1. Correction of problems
    a. *Verify that the problem exists.* Does the statement of the problem and supporting documentation show that the actual results differ from the expected results? Often, the user will come to the maintainer or consultant with what he feels is a problem. Upon examination, very often the user's manual will give a sufficient explanation. Sometimes it doesn't, but the requirements will, in which case the user's manual may need to be modified. A large percentage of "problems" can be disposed of in this manner.
    b. *Isolate the problem.* Isolation of the problem involves using the available information to determine where in the program the problem is most likely to exist. For this stage of program or system maintenance, a good overview of the system and the tools available for gathering information about it is mandatory. The specific pieces that may be involved in the occurrence of the problem must be identified. In some cases, where specific information is necessary but does not exist, it can prove very useful to create a tool to obtain it. The tool thus created can (with some forethought) be used when that *type* of information is required again. Given the proper tools, it is likely that one or more runs of the failing program will be necessary to gather needed information. (Were the program results correct at point A? Point B? . . .) Analysis of such results should pinpoint the program error.

c. *Reproduce the problem.* Assuming that the problem is
real and isolated, and assuming further that no intuitive
leap has brought forth a solution, further help is needed.
In a large system, it may be important to create a tiny test
case which exhibits the problem characteristics—that is,
it is a   reproduction of the problem, but in a more
manageable way. Strip away all the nonpertinent information (often called "garbage") that surrounds the
problem data, and isolate it to its most simple form. If
traces or other debug information are needed, for
example, it would be preferable to obtain only output in
an area relevant to the problem at hand, and not a ream
of paper most of which pertained to aspects of the failing
input case not relevant to the problem. Often this specific
test case can then be added to the collection of system
regression tests.

3.2.2.5   EVOLUTION VERSUS REVOLUTION

The process of maintenance may be either evolutionary or
revolutionary. If a large software system has existed over a long period
of time, fills a purpose with minor "bugs" appearing from time to time
(but in the main, running as it should and being used by many people),
and is reasonably easy to understand, then most likely it is possible to
evolve the system further into a better system. If, on the other hand, the
system has unpredictable production-run characteristics, or unex-
plainable spaghetti-twisted code, more immediate surgery may be
necessary.

Parts of a system may exhibit both of these characteristics (i.e.,
both well modularized and hodge-podged, "kludged" sections of
code), and thus different tacks may be taken within the same system. If
the design is such that the underlying philosophy is wrong, "revolutionary" surgery is likely to have to be performed (i.e., the module
totally redone from scratch).

In cases where the system has grown, little pieces being added as
they were bumped into, then most likely an evolutionary approach
should be taken. Old-style code usually exhibits many GOTOs,

frequent reference to global flags which the previous builder has resorted to in order to add special cases, and so on.

For example, one large and complex piece of code performed six functions that had a high degree of commonality. The flow through the code was essentially from beginning to end, but some of the functions were so different that the code hopped out of line in many cases, continued with the special circumstances, and then reentered the main flow at a subsequent point. Needless to say, this code was extremely difficult to follow and was nearly impossible to modify without adding more flag checking. This code was modified slowly over a period of years to exist as modularized pieces. The six major functions each proceeded in a straightforward fashion through the code, calling subordinate procedures or functions as necessary. The subordinate functions were common to all, with the differences in processing clearly defined between the calls to the common modules. As a result of this evolution, it was possible to introduce changes in each of the six functions in a manner which assured that none of the other five was affected.

3.2.3 Documentation

Rarely does software documentation contain the kinds of information necessary for maintaining a program. The documents, when they do exist, are generally written to conform to a separate set of requirements which specify what the software documentation is to contain. All too frequently, these requirements provide for irrelevant or useless information and omit the kinds of information that the maintainer *really* needs. So, in a real sense the document, which is supposed to be a clarifying piece of material, ends up obscuring the needed information.

Because documentation is separate from the software product itself, it is also frequently out of date. Ideally, the document would be a perfect reflection of the program. In actual fact, this is rarely, if ever, true. The documentation can therefore be misleading. Who in their right mind would attempt to make corrections to a program after reading only the program documentation and not the listing?

This book therefore recommends the heresy that the listing be the place where most software documentation is placed. Nearly every requirement for documentation describing a program can be met and in fact probably exceeded by requiring the same information in the listing. (This position is discussed further in section 4.3.)

3.2.3.1   HISTORIC DOCUMENTATION

Software documentation methodology has traditionally ignored historic documentation. Historic documentation is typically informally prepared information used for a particular phase of product development. It includes the following categories:

1. *Design notes.* The most important form of historic documentation is comprised of the design notes (these are over and above the formal design, as represented by program design language or flowcharts). These usually handwritten notes are irreplaceable, particularly when the maintainer needs to modify an area and wants to understand *why* the existing design evolved as it did. Most contemporary documentation does not provide for this piece of history. Some of this material may be prepared formally, for an initial or overview document, but the authors suggest preserving as much of it as possible in its original form, and filing it chronologically. Sections of material pertaining to the same subject can be cross-indexed, by adding some sort of page numbering to the design file, and building an index referencing those page numbers. One reason the design note approach is not usually formally required is that design notes often grow obsolete as an implementation evolves. Essential to the use of design notes is either (1) an understanding that they provide good overview but not good detail, or (2) a commitment to keeping them up to date. The former is the usual method. The latter, perhaps even with publication of designs being required, may be the way of the future.

2. *Problem reports.* A (probably) chronological file of problems as they are reported, numbered to allow easy tracking, should be kept. They should remain in a working file until they are

closed out, then placed into a historic file. (Part of this process may lend itself to automation, with data being extracted from the individual reports to appear in summary and/or list form.) These historic records should also be kept in their original form (and not retyped), since some information could be lost in transliteration. Although these files will not be referenced often, when they are needed they are *very* needed (perhaps to assist in the isolation and correction of a similar error).

3. *Improvement suggestions.* Another vital piece of historical data is a collection of *ideas* for later improvements to the program. Such ideas often emerge in two flavors: major improvements (which the authors call "partly baked ideas") and cosmetic improvements. The latter are usually scribbled onto the listing, incorporated in an upcoming version, and forgotten; but the former, which typically arise while the maintainer is immersed in some other work, should be collected in a central location (folder or binder) that will be browsed through periodically. This both prevents good ideas from being irrevocably lost, and provides material the maintainer's manager or customer may want to evaluate in the future.

4. *Version description*—release notices. This very important piece of documentation is often overlooked. Every release or version of the software product should have a complete description of the changes that were incorporated into the product. This includes a list of the problem reports that have been closed, a verbal description of the change, and a description, where possible, of the impact on the user in the user's terms. User's manual and documentation manual documentation changes should also be referenced here.

Note that none of these forms of documentation are part of what tradition has dictated programmers must write; and yet note that these are very important forms of documentation. Note also that in many cases, this documentation is better kept in handwritten, informal form than prepared more formally. Clarity and spontaneity of the original thought process is all too frequently lost in such transliteration.

3.3 REFERENCES

1. "Structured Programming in a Production Programming Environment," Proceedings of the IEEE International Conference on Reliable Software, 1975; Baker.

   Discusses structured coding and programming standards in the context of the structured programming methodology.

2. "Standard Compiler Workshop Final Report," Eglin Air Force Base, 1978; Bladen.

   A summary of the results of a workshop to define the environment for the Ada programming language. Four study groups focused on (1) an operation plan, (2) specifications and verification/validation, (3) optimization, and (4) software support tools. The latter proposes a specific set of tools to support Ada.

3. "Software Engineering," IEEE Transactions on Computers, December 1976; Boehm.

   Defines software engineering and constituent parts. Discusses costs and trends. Section VII, Software Maintenance, says that maintenance accounts for about 70% of the cost of software and is a "highly neglected activity."

4. *Characteristics of Software Quality,* North-Holland, 1978; Boehm, Brown, Kaspar, Lipow, MacLeod, and Merritt.

   Discusses maintainability as one element of quality. Shows a functional breakdown of maintainability into a tree structure of constituent parts. Presents positive and negative maintainability characteristics.

5. "Software Production Data," RADC-TR-77-177, 1977; Carter, Donahoo, Farquhar, and Hurt.

   Describes research performed by Computer Sciences Corp. to assess the effects of "modern programming practices" (MPP). Defines the "threads" concept as a way of tracking requirements through the subsequent phases of the software life cycle, and assesses its actual use on various projects. The impact of elements of MPP on the software life cycle, and on common error types, is estimated.

6. "Hints on Test Data Selection: Help for the Practicing Programmer," Computer, April 1978; DeMillo, Lipton, and Sayward.

   Makes a strong case for the use of an intuitive, ad hoc approach to testing, on the grounds that other approaches reject the truism that most programs under test are "nearly correct."

7. "Make—A Program for Maintaining Computer Programs," Software Practice and Experience, April 1979; Feldman.

   Describes a version control tool that runs on the UNIX operating system.

8. "E-3A Software Maintenance," Proceedings of the AIAA Conference on Computers in Aerospace, 1977; Fox.

   Describes maintenance activities on a Department of Defense command and control project. Discusses the E-3A project itself, the management structure for software maintenance, and the activities involved.

9. "The New Software Economics," Computerworld, January 8, 1979 and subsequent issues; Frank.

   Sees a new role for proprietary software products in the typical installation mix of software acquisition. Describes the future of software productivity improvement as "bleak." Says "the ultimate factor in software productivity is the capability of the individual software practitioner."

10. "A Verification Case Study," Proceedings of the AIAA Computers in Aerospace Conference, 1977; Gannon.

    Describes the JOVIAL Automated Verification System (JAVS) and its use. The self-test of JAVS using JAVS as part of its government acceptance testing is discussed. Conclusions about the effectiveness of test coverage analyzers are drawn.

11. "Evaluation of Maintenance Software in Real-Time Systems," IEEE Transactions on Computers, June 1978; Gay.

    Describes a real-time "trouble locating program" which relies on error seeding (the deliberate introduction of known errors) to evaluate the number of errors in software.

12. "Testing Maintainability," ACM SIGSOFT Software Engineering Notes, April 1979; Gelperin.

    Suggests techniques oriented to evaluating software maintainability: standards auditing, "what if" analysis (to anticipate future change), structural evaluation (to better understand product cohesion and complexity), and production testing.

13.   "Observations of Fallibility in Applications of Modern Programming Methodologies," IEEE Transactions on Software Engineering, 1976; Gerhart and Yelowitz.

Describes errors in software developed by modern techniques and thought to be correct. Recommends (1) better analysis of the complete task, (2) applying a breadth of reliability techniques, (3) avoiding preconceived notions of "hard" and "easy" (easy is often more error-prone), (4) not confusing good structure with correctness, and (5) understanding that new methodologies are not panaceas.

14.   *Software Reliability Guidebook,* Prentice-Hall, 1979, Glass.

Surveys techniques for achieving software reliability. Discusses the interrelationship between reliability and maintenance. Describes a variety of tools and methodologies that can assist in making software more reliable.

15.   "Of Flat Earths and Flowcharts," *The Power of Peonage,* Computing Trends, 1979; Glass.

Describes a humorous (hypothetical) happening that occurred as the flowcharting era ended.

16.   "MAIDS Study—Program Testing and Diagnosis Technology," Letter Report N/000-6-73, 1973; Goodenough and Eanes.

Discusses the inadequacy of testing and the importance of early detection of design errors. Includes regression testing in a general discussion of testing strategies.

17.   "The Advanced Interactive Debugging System (AIDS)," ACM SIG-PLAN Notices, December 1979; Hart.

Describes a commercial (Sperry Univac) debugging system which is symbolic, language-independent, and does not require preplanned debug code inclusion.

18.   "Specifying Software Requirements for Complex Systems: New Techniques and Their Application," Proceedings of the IEEE 1979 Specifications of Reliable Software Conference; Heninger.

Describes the use of formal requirements specifications in the context of a trouble-plagued software maintenance project. Provides realistic large-project approaches and solutions.

19.   "An Evaluation of the Effectiveness of Symbolic Testing," Software Practice and Experience, July 1978; Howden.

Evaluates several different debugging methodologies on their ability to detect errors. Finds symbolic testing particularly promising. Also studies test coverage analyzers of differing degrees of rigor, and other strategies.

20. "An Approach to Program Testing," ACM Computing Surveys, September 1975; Huang.

Tutorial paper that analyzes the difficulties of rigorous testing, suggests the test coverage analyzer concept as a solution, and discusses the usage, strengths, and weaknesses of such a tool.

21. "The Programmer's Workbench," The Bell System Technical Journal, July-August 1978; Dolotta, Haight and Mashey.

Describes a tools environment which functions under the UNIX operating system. Usage of the system, implementation problems, and lessons learned are described.

22. *Principles of Program Design,* Academic Press, 1975; Jackson.

Takes a problem-oriented approach to design concepts—each concept is followed by a problem solution illustrating the concept. Problems are taken from the data processing realm, and sample code is in COBOL. Data structure design is stressed.

23. *Software Tools,* Addison Wesley, 1976; Kernighan and Plauger.

Describes tools, their value to the programmer, and the kinds of tools which may be useful.

24. *The Elements of Programming Style,* McGraw-Hill, 1978; Kernighan and Plauger.

Presents a definition of good programming style by means of a set of about 100 rules augmented by examples and discussion. Elaborates such ideas as "Modularize—use subroutines," "Let the data structure the program," and "Don't comment bad code—rewrite it."

25. "Air Force Command and Control Information Processing in the 1980s; Trends in Software Technology," R-1012-PR, The Rand Corp., 1974; Kosy.

Describes the evolution and postulated future of software in command and control technology. Puts technological concepts into perspective, including HOL usage and benefits.

26. "Debugging Techniques," Software Practice and Experience, January 1979; Lauesen.

Describes ten techniques for improving debugging—top-down debug, test output creation, self-testing programs, an approach to test data selection, independent tests, acceptance testing, configuration management of tests, test-result recording, device simulation, bug record keeping.

27. *Programming Proverbs for Fortran Programmers,* Hayden, 1975; Ledgard.

Represents programming style as a series of "proverbs" or rules. This book contains Fortran rules; Ledgard has written other books for other languages.

28. "Characteristics of Application Software Maintenance," Communications of the ACM, June 1978; Lientz, Swanson, and Tompkins.

Surveys 69 computing installations to identify the characteristics of software maintenance. Studies largely COBOL-oriented environments with high ongoing maintenance needs.

29. "On the Development of Large Reliable Programs," *Current Trends in Programming Methodology,* Prentice-Hall, 1977; Linger and Mills.

Advocates structured programming as a tool for coding "error-free" programs; uses illustrative examples.

30. "Software Quality Assurance," Computer, August 1979; Miller.

A compendium of articles on experience with a variety of software quality assurance techniques.

31. *Reliable Software through Composite Design,* Petrocelli/Charter, 1975; Myers.

Advocates modularity, if done properly, as the key to effective software development. Describes proper modularizing—how to design them, how to interrelate them. Stresses the importance of the design phase.

32. "Module Design and Coding," *Software Reliability,* Wiley-Interscience, 1976; Myers.

Stresses the importance of high-level language. Also discusses structured coding, standards, and other coding techniques.

33. "A Controlled Experiment in Program Testing and Code Walkthroughs/Inspections," Communications of the ACM, September 1978; Myers.

Describes an experiment in error seeking using testing and code review. Sees these techniques as complementary, with both being necessary.

34. *Composite/Structured Design,* Van Nostrand Reinhold, 1978; Myers.

     Enhances the ref. [31] discussion of modularity by providing objective criteria for evaluating it. Talks about functional strength modules and data coupling.

35. "A 1900 Fortran Post Mortem Dump System," Software Practice and Experience, July 1978; Ng and Young.

     Describes a source language debug tool which produces Fortran language dumps (optionally) on program termination. Includes symbolically identified data and some execution history data. Interfaces with the compiler, linker and a post-mortem-dump analyzer.

36. "Research toward Ways of Improving Software Maintenance," ESD-TR-73-125, 1973; Overton, Colin, and Tillman.

     Describes an experiment in which software maintenance activities were measured. Contains many quotes from maintenance programmers. Stresses the structure ("conceptual groupings") of the software. Defines specific maintainability techniques, and a maintainability check list. Discusses use of a graphics terminal to support maintenance.

37. "Software Testing: Principles and Practice Using a Testing Coverage Analyzer," Transactions of the Software '77 Conference, October 1977; Paige.

     Testing is called "the most practical means to demonstrate software correctness." The notion of a testing analyzer is defined and illustrated, with sample analyzer outputs shown. Testing strategies using an analyzer are discussed.

38. "Automatic Software Test Drivers," Computer, April 1978; Panzl.

     Discusses regression testing ("under present technology, effective regression testing is seldom possible") in the context of an automatic system for producing and retaining test procedures.

39. "On the Criteria to Be Used in Decomposing Systems into Modules," Communications of the ACM, December 1972; Parnas.

     Uses an example to discuss two strategies for defining modules. Recommends modularizing to promote "information hiding," such that modules contain design decisions which are likely to change.

40. "The Influence of Software Structure on Reliability," Proceedings of IEEE International Conference on Reliable Software, 1975; Parnas.

     Distinguishes between reliability (delivering usable services) and correctness (meeting specifications). Emphasizes the importance of the former and stresses modularizing to promote it. Poses questions pertinent to module definition.

41. "Department of Defense Requirements for the Programming Environment for the Common High Order Language," January 1979; Pebbleman revised.

    See ref. [51] for a later version of this document.

42. "Notes on the Design of Euclid," Proceedings of an ACM Conference on Language Design for Reliable Software, 1977; Popek, Horning, Lampson, Mitchell, and London.

    Describes a language for writing system programs, called Euclid, which stresses capabilities for verification. Contains a good discussion on the Euclid philosophy of module/cluster definition.

43. "A Production Environment Evaluation of Interactive Programming," U.S. Army Computer Systems Command Technical Documentary Report USA CSC-AT-74-03, 1974; Reaser, Priesman, and Gill.

    Describes an evaluation of interactive versus batch software development. Both productivity and cost were found to be significantly improved using timesharing.

44. "A Glossary of Software Tools and Techniques," Computer (IEEE), July 1977; Reifer and Trattner.

    Divides software tools into six categories—simulation, development, test and evaluation, operations and maintenance, performance measurement, programming support. Lists 70 types of tools, categorizing them as noted above.

45. "The UNIX Time-Sharing System," The Bell System Technical Journal, July-August 1978; Ritchie and Thompson.

    Describes the UNIX interactive operating system, both its user interface and its implementation. The concept of the pipe, an interprocess data communication mechanism, is covered, along with the other unique features of the system.

46. "Higher Order Languages for Avionics Software—A Survey, Summary and Critique," NAECON 1978; Rubey.

    Traces the history of avionics (real-time) HOL usage. Cites problems and resolutions in HOL versus assembler trade-offs. Sees trends leading toward more HOL usage, especially because of increased ability to support change during maintenance.

47. "Timesharing vs. Batch Processing, the Experimental Evidence," Proceedings of the 1968 Spring Joint Computer Conference; Sackman.

Summarizes the pros and cons of timesharing usage and the results of five experimental studies. Study results tend to show (1) less human cost for timesharing, (2) more computer cost, and (3) programmer preference for timesharing.

48. "The Problem of Programming Communication with Changing Machines—A Proposed Solution," Communications of the ACM, August 1958; Share Ad-Hoc Committee on Universal Languages (Strong, Wegstein, Tritter, Olsztyn, Mack, and Steel).

The earliest known definition of the UNCOL (Universal Computer-Oriented Language) concept. UNCOL was to be the intermediate language into which all HOLs (then called POLs, from Problem-Oriented Languages) would be translated, and from which all machine languages (ML) would be generated.

49. "Programming Tools: Statement Counts and Procedure Timings," SIGPLAN Notices, December 1978; Sites.

Advocates the use of software analysis tools to obtain visibility for making programs more efficient.

50. "Software Acquisition Management Guidebook, Software Maintenance Volume," System Development Corp. TM-5772/004/02, November 1977; Stanfield and Skrukrud.

Describes "preventing maintenance" techniques throughout the software life cycle. Specifically directed toward DoD-procured software, but applies to all. Provides ideas and checklists for maintenance-oriented software review. Summarizes DoD regulations, specifications, and standards relevant to software maintenance.

51. "Requirements for Ada Programming Support Environments," February 1980, "Stoneman."

One in a series of iterations leading to the definition of a common tool environment for the Department of Defense Ada language.

52. "Automatic Generation of Self-Metric Software," IEEE Symposium on Computer Software Reliability, 1973; Stucki.

Summarizes approaches used to monitor software, and describes the Program Evaluator and Tester (PET) tool for gathering operational data on program performance—statement frequency counts, max/min values of data, and so on.

53.   "New Directions in Automated Tools for Improving Software Quality," *Current Trends in Programming Methodology,* Prentice-Hall, 1977; Stucki.

Describes assertion checking, a debugging technique by means of which a program can detect its own errors.

54.   "The Dimensions of Maintenance," Proceedings of the 2nd International Conference on Software Engineering, 1976; Swanson.

Proposes to define theoretical bases of software maintenance. Defines corrective, adaptive, and perfective maintenance. Suggests the contents of a maintenance data base, and measure of maintenance performance. Recommends further research into the subject.

55.   "Guidelines for Software Portability," Software Practice and Experience, November 1978; Tanenbaum, Klint, and Bohm.

Pitfalls to the production of portable software are described. They are categorized into problems of (1) programming languages, (2) floating-point numbers, (3) files, (4) physical media, (5) interactive terminal I/O, (6) operating systems, (7) machine architecture, and (8) documentation. Specifics are discussed.

56.   "UNIX Time-sharing System," The Bell System Technical Journal, July 1978.

Over a dozen articles on the capabilities, development, and maintenance of UNIX, generally acknowledged to be at the forefront of operating system technology. Includes a discussion of the suite of development/maintenance tools known as the "Programmer's Workbench."

57.   "Program Standards Help Software Maintainability," 1978 Proceedings of the Annual Reliability and Maintainability Symposium; White.

Evaluates the impact of software standards on maintainability. Concludes that modularity, structured coding, and in-line commentary have merit.

58.   "Beyond Programming Languages," Communications of the ACM, July 1979; Winograd.

Suggests that current programming language concepts are inadequate for the complex problems increasingly often being solved. Proposes the concept of a higher-level language that emphasizes declarations of known facts rather than imperative statements.

59. "Languages and Structured Programs," *Current Trends in Programming Methodology,* Prentice-Hall, 1977; Wulf.

Discusses the "software crisis," the need for structure in programs, and the role of languages in providing it. Stresses newly emerging language concepts.

60. *Programming with Ada: An Introduction by Means of Graduated Examples,* Prentice-Hall, 1980; Wegner.

Introduces the Department of Defense language Ada. Describes its content from a programmer point of view. Starts with a simple description, and adds complexity later. Emphasizes examples.

Four

The Management Side of Maintenance

The manager of a software maintenance effort—and almost all software managers inevitably are responsible for some maintenance— must deal with a collection of real problems with sometimes unreal overtones.

For instance, as we have seen, there is the folklore (i.e., maintenance is a dull, uncreative task to be staffed by the lowest-ranking team member) and the fact (inept maintenance can quickly wreck an originally well developed piece of software). And there are beliefs (e.g., software managers are usually content with the technical quality of software maintenance [23]) that conflict with realities (maintenance, as a microcosm of the whole software development cycle, is only as good as—or as bad as—the original development process).

In fact, there are some basic misunderstandings of the entire maintenance process. Many managers, pressed for a figure, would guess that maintenance consumes a small fraction of their technologists' time—say 20%. They would also guess that most of that maintenance time would be spent correcting errors in the code—

perhaps 80%. As we have already seen, they would be dead wrong.

The literature on software maintenance is still pretty sparse. But what there is, is pretty consistent. Study after study has shown that maintenance consumes 50 to 80% of software costs and time [3, 23]. A smaller number of studies, with comparable consistency, say that error correction is a minor part of the maintainer's job—down at the 15 to 40% level [23]. The aware software maintenance manager should be asking himself the question: "What are all of those people doing for all of that time?" It is the intention of this book to answer that question. The question then follows: "What should and/or can I do about that?" This chapter is intended to help with the answer to that. (A good overview of the entire software management task as actually practiced in the field is found in ref. [21].)

4.1   PLANNING FOR MAINTENANCE

The people side of maintenance, as portrayed in chapter 2, is the manager's chief problem area in planning for maintenance. "Who can I pick to maximize the continued quality of my already developed software? Who is best psychologically fitted to stand up to the traditional negative stigma attached to maintenance? Who is flexible enough to adjust to the existing coding style of my programs without having to rip them up and start over? Who understands the importance of, and can facilitate the continued existence of, good maintenance-oriented code and maintenance-oriented documentation?"

There are plenty of I-questions for the maintenance manager to answer as well. "How can I be sure of the quality of my maintainer's work? How can I maximize the quantity of useful work my maintainers perform? How can I get better visibility into the whole process? At what points in the process should I impose management control? What kind should I impose? How can I balance the work to be done with the budgeted dollars available in a software world rampant with estimating unknowns?" These are hard questions. Like all other management questions, they are best answered by hard-headed managers who have educated and experienced intuitions. The key phrase here is "educated intuition." The manager who understands the maintenance process intimately is best able to plan for its quantitative and qualitative success.

4.1.1 Planning for High-Quantity Maintenance: The Importance of People

It has already been seen that the personnel requirements for top-notch maintenance personnel are surprisingly severe. Obtaining people who are flexible, resistant to derision, capable and creative, and good documentors is like a line from a very old song: "I'm looking for a man who plays alto and saxophone, and doubles on the clarinet, and wears a size 37 suit." But satisfying those requirements is a first essential to all that follows in managing to achieve good maintenance of software. "The prime factor affecting the reliability of software is the selection, motivation and management of the personnel who design and maintain it" [6]. The importance of a few good people—or a lot of good people, if necessary—is all too easily overlooked, especially in a world chronically short of software-skilled people. When your installation is functioning far short of the number of skilled people it needs, it is tempting to lower the barriers and hire underskilled people. That may be necessary and even, done with care, wise; but do not assign, willy-nilly, your personnel leftovers (new hires or otherwise) to maintenance. The resulting chaos may end up consuming you. Maximization of the quantity of maintenance performed by those assigned to maintenance tasks is like a venture into management never-never land. The theme will recur in this book that managers traditionally have happily and quickly escaped from the details of programming technology, and that that in itself has caused a multitude of software problems. Especially in the domain of high quantity and quality maintenance, this is a severe problem. The maintainer spends all day every day poking around in the innards of someone's code. Is his or her time well spent? Without having some understanding of the nature of that code, how can the manager ever judge?

It was mentioned earlier that software maintainers spend only 15 to 40% of their time correcting actual errors in the code. Obviously, the question of what they do with the remainder of their time is critical to the quantity of work performed by a maintenance team. So, too, as we will see, is the question of how they spend the actual error-correction time.

One study [23] of software maintenance breaks down the maintainer's time as follows:

17% corrective
18% adaptive
60% perfective
5% other

Perfective maintenance is the big shocker of the lot—the least understood, most time-consuming facet of maintenance. Stated succinctly, it's just "make the software better." That can range anywhere from user enhancements (e.g., putting a newly developed trajectory algorithm into an existing space shot program), to programmer improvement (e.g., structuring a previously tangled and unmaintainable piece of code), to documentation updates (e.g., making the user's manual more user-readable). What is surprising here is that this is where the maintenance dollar goes, and the manager of software maintenance must come to an understanding of perfective maintenance if he is to manage the quantitative aspects of software maintenance. There is a temptation on the part of many managers—particularly those who have left their technology behind—to try to eliminate perfective maintenance. After all, in one fell swoop 60% of the consumer of 50 to 80% of your software dollar is thereby eliminated. But this is a dangerous and naive temptation. Granted, there is a touch of the mad scientist in every technologist, fiddling with the symbolic dials on his newly created software robot, tuning it to unneeded perfection—but perfective maintenance, for all of that, is still necessary. The cost of the future fixes and enhancements is driven down by proper perfective maintenance; and perhaps more important, so is the response time for those future changes. The ability to satisfy tomorrow's time-constrained change request may well be dependent on today's perfective maintenance work. The very fact that managers tend to be satisfied with software maintenance as a whole is probably intimately related to the fact that responsible programmers have traditionally performed a good level of perfective maintenance.

The message here, then, is not to truncate perfective maintenance, but to obtain visibility into it and control it as necessary. And that, of course, is equally true of adaptive and corrective maintenance.

Now, visibility and control are obviously essential to maximizing the quantity of software maintenance performed. The question is: How much visibility and how much control? (Methods of gaining visibility and control will be treated in a later section.) Probably the hardest question in the whole of management methodology is how to control, and how much. It is a hard question because there is no precise answer. And there is no precise answer because it is a very individual-dependent issue (see, for example, ref. [2]). Some programmers can function well only in an environment with maximum management control—their sense of responsibility simply must be nudged by management action. Others, however, are offended and demotivated by management control. Their sense of responsibility is sufficient, most or all of the time, to guarantee a kind of internal control. These facts of human existence present the ultimate managerial dilemma— how to manage and control fairly while metering out different levels of control to different people. To a large extent, most software managers are unable to resolve this dilemma—some rule all their employees with a harsh and controlling hand, whereas others manage so loosely as to lose all visibility and control. These homogeneous approaches, or perhaps a compromise approach somewhere in between, may be necessary and even desirable in the world of software development, especially in the large-project environment. But in the maintenance world, where programmer traits are so interrelated with performance, they will simply not work.

The emphasis of the maintenance manager eager to maximize individual performance must be

1. To understand the capabilities and responsibilities of the person.
2. To maintain visibility and control consistent with that understanding.
3. To convince the employees working in this uneven-handed environment that the manager is dealing fairly and consistently with all.

And that is a tall order for the software manager.

Now, how does the alert software manager maximize the quantitative output of his whole staff?

1. By effective, individualized control of his people. This has been elaborated above.

2. By understanding the tasks they are doing. This means knowing what changes are being worked, why they are being worked, and what the impact of that work is (including some level of knowledge of the code to be changed).

3. By controlling the tasks themselves. This means change control, and it will be discussed in a subsequent section.

4. By providing an environment that facilitates the maintainer in doing his job. This, too, will be discussed later.

With this approach the manager can distinguish (or ignore the distinction, if he is wise) among corrective, adaptive, and perfective maintenance. Properly controlled, in spite of the surprising statistics, all of these facets of maintenance are valid and productive portions of the overall software maintenance task. This answer to the question of maximizing the quantity of maintenance work done is perhaps disturbingly subjective. It is like answering a question with a question. But the fact of the matter is that there is no better objective answer available. Management is and always will be an art of applied intuition. If objective answers to these kinds of questions were available, management might even be unnecessary.

4.1.2   Planning for High-Quality Maintenance: Reviews and Audits

The preceding discussion of the quantity of maintenance performance placed a heavy emphasis on the care and feeding of the individual maintainer. The amount of total work performed, it was argued, is heavily person-dependent. Visibility and control mechanisms to maximize quantity should acknowledge and, in fact, take advantage of human differences.

That same emphasis must underlie the achievement of high-*quality* software maintenance as well. For all of the reasons stated previously, the carefully selected, well-managed, capable, and responsible pro-grammer is the best component of a high-quality and high-quantity maintenance team. Without that component, the manager's task is infinitely more complex, since he must somehow try to inject those missing entities, like intravenous feedings, into an ill software main-tenance body.

But there is more to achieving high-quality software maintenance than careful selection and management of a team of individuals. The quality of the product can only be judged by looking at the product itself. The manager must provide for a review and audit process which oversees the maintenance effort.

In some ways, this is a forbidden topic. Technologists are sus-picious of external examination of their seemingly personal propri-etary programs. Managers are leery of requirements imposed upon them to judge technical facets of a product they have sometimes chosen to be ill equipped to judge. Thus, although many references and standards manuals [5, 13, 25, 39] pay lip service to or even enact the principle of external review of software products, this technology has seldom if ever affected the maintenance phase of software production.

How can the negative impacts of this forbidden topic be dealt with? (It is fairly obvious that the quality of software products in a maintenance phase is at least as important as their quality during the development phase, and thus few would argue conceptually against the use of reviews and audits during maintenance.) To alleviate the technologists' fears, staff the review/audit heavily with capable technical peers. The process should be a knowledgeable review of all of the quality goals to be met by a product change, including such intricately evaluated goals as product efficiency; and only technical peers will be capable of performing that kind of analysis. Prepare the review/audit participants to create a positive, we're-all-in-this-together kind of approach, and discourage or eliminate those who are incapable of tact or are overly defensive. And make the formality of the review match the importance of the task. Trivial changes can even be self-reviewed. Small changes might be reviewed by two people. Only the momentous ones need a formally convened, carefully controlled review atmosphere.

So much for the technologist's concerns. Now for the manager's. Hopefully, by now you understand the dichotomy between the need for a review conducted by technically knowledgeable people and the typical software manager's technical skill level. They simply don't mesh. The manager, subconsciously or consciously aware of this fact, traditionally has either (1) not allowed reviews or audits; (2) participated in them, forcing their content to cover areas he understands; or (3) opted out. None of these is the right answer.

Options 1 and 2 are obviously wrong. If the quality of the delivered software product is to be maximized, it obviously must be evaluated, not avoided. The manager who boasts of "on schedule, within budget" software has, perhaps without realizing it, omitted consideration of product quality, which is of course at least as important as schedule/ budget considerations. The manager who attends a review but concentrates on top-level considerations is performing two-thirds of a valid service, but he is also thwarting the remaining one-third.

Option 3 is more attractive, but also wrong. *Some* reviews, of course, are purely technology-oriented and should not include managers. But software maintenance product quality reviews demand that management considerations be one factor of the review process.

The right answer here is for the manager to participate in the review process, contributing when he can contribute, quietly reabsorbing his rusty technology [15] when he cannot. Thus, the manager remains knowledgeable of the quality of the product for which he is responsible, and refurbishes his skills at the same time.

Quality of software maintenance, then, depends on the same techniques needed for high-quantity software maintenance—and on a good review/audit process in addition. Good people plus a well-evaluated product—those are the management methods for assuring high quality in software maintenance.

4.1.3   Other Planning Considerations

It is an oversimplification of software maintenance planning to imply that ensuring high quantity and quality will result in a totally satisfactory software maintenance effort. Some other very real constraints are placed upon the software maintenance manager. He has a finite budget which can only sustain a certain level of manning and computer time. He has schedules—either self-imposed or originating on the outside—which determine when some or all maintenance is to be done. He has support facilities: computers, peripherals, aides, and clerks who can sustain certain levels of activity and no more. He has an organization that either enhances his ability to maintain software, or thwarts it. And he has documentation, both to assist in the maintenance effort and to produce as an end product.

All of these factors must be planned for—elaborately, if the software product is huge and complex, or in passing if the software is trivial. Acquiring adequate computer support for maintenance, for example, can vary from the need to build a new building to house a newly ordered computer [15], to using the development computer with no incremental resource requirements at all.

The key thought here is "planning," and the adjective implied is "advanced." All of the quantity/quality/resource/budget/scheduling/organizational/documentation considerations must be begun prior to the start of maintenance of the software. This is not to say that such planning is easy—remember that management is the art of educated intuition, and remember, too, that software estimates are notoriously bad. But software efforts, including maintenance, are only as good as the foresight that goes into them.

This section has not tried to provide guidelines for budgeting or scheduling. Primarily, this is because such concerns are similar to the same concerns for software developmental projects, and quite a bit has already been written on that subject (e.g., [8,11]), much of it unfortunately (and usually admittedly) of highly debatable value. Experience has shown that budgeting/scheduling is almost entirely a factor of specific project-experienced intuition, with education's role in enhancing that intuition still unclear. (One software maintenance project mentioned in the literature, for example, was originally staffed with over 100 people and proved to require 41 more [12]!)

The issues of organization for, and documentation of, software maintenance can be profitably dealt with, however. The following sections expand on those concepts.

4.2 ORGANIZATION FOR MAINTENANCE

It has already been pointed out that software maintenance is a microcosm of the whole software development process. A software fix or a software change requires requirements definition, design, coding, testing, and of course follow-on maintenance of its own. (Thus, software maintenance is a recursively defined process.) It is not surprising, then, that in its organizational aspects, software maintenance demands all the consideration of software development. In fact, in many software organizations, maintenance is carried out in tandem with development activities, often within the development organizational structure. In an extreme case—and this is not at all uncommon or necessarily undesirable—maintenance is provided by development programmers, sandwiching it in among their ongoing development tasks, on a sort of human timesharing basis. Programmer A may be implementing system Z while retaining maintenance responsibility for system Y, which he probably developed.

At the other extreme (and this is also not uncommon or necessarily undesirable), there may be an entirely separate organizational structure set aside purely for the purpose of maintaining software. Programmers A, B, and C develop the software, pass the completed software through some sort of acceptance/delivery window, and turn control over to programmers X, Y, and Z for maintenance. In this situation, programmer X may be responsible for maintaining parts or all of several software systems.

In between these extremes lies the umbrella software organizational concept, where maintenance is one organizational entity under the umbrella of software development. Programmers may be doing only maintenance, only development, or some combination of the two—and because of the close organizational linkage, transition from one of these phases to another is easy and common.

The key considerations in choosing among these options are the flexibility of the organization's programming staff and the complexity of the software to be maintained. If the entire staff disdains maintenance activities, for instance, it may be wise to sprinkle the maintenance activities broadly and evenly on all of them; if some of the staff enjoy maintenance and are flexible and capable enough to do it well, on the other hand, a separate maintenance organization may be preferable. Overriding or at least operating in tandem with these human considerations, however, are two more goal-oriented criteria: the complexity of the software and the priority of the maintenance activity. If the software is extremely complex—such as a large operating system or a shop scheduling application, for example—it may be vital to retain some or all of the original development team for maintenance consultation or for the maintenance itself. Under these circumstances, the "human timesharing" concept may work best—the original development team has probably moved on to a new development project, but they should also retain responsibility for maintaining the old.

On the other hand, if the priority of the maintenance activity is high—a payroll system or a real-time system would be good examples —then it is probably organizationally desirable to separate off that maintenance into a separate organization in order to focus on rapid and accurate maintenance activities.

This obviously leaves caught in the middle the class of software that is both complex and of high priority. If it is complex, the developer should maintain it; but if its priority is high, a separate organization is preferable! The resolution of this dilemma is left as a case-by-case exercise for the manager reading this book. It is difficult decisions such as these that exercise and test that educated intuition which we discussed earlier.

No attempt will be made here to define organizational options open to the software development organization. Instead, those special organizational considerations that are imposed by maintenance activities will be dealt with and tied in where appropriate to the development or maintenance organization structure. For example, the dichotomy between technology-led organizations (e.g., chief-programmer teams [5, 39]) and administratively led organizations (e.g., the traditional organizational hierarchic tree structure [6, 12, 30, 35]) will not be dealt with here. The references are provided for those interested in pursuing those kinds of concepts, however.

The remainder of this section will discuss special organizational considerations that should be given to software maintenance. It is organized by function to be performed; at the end of the discussion some possible organizational structures will be defined.

4.2.1   Change Board

First and foremost on any software maintenance project is a review of the question: "Is the change really needed?" The complexity of this question may range from the trivial (e.g., the payroll checks are all high by $1000, in which case a change is obviously needed) to the extremely difficult (e.g., a customer has requested that a name field be expanded from 30 characters to 35 characters, which has major repercussions on file and report formats and internal data declarations and/or processing procedures and thus must be subject to cost/benefit analysis). Note that the complexity of the question is largely unrelated to its importance—of the two examples given above, the trivial one is obviously more important than the difficult one.

There are two vital and sometimes contradictory requirements for a change evaluation process: fast response when the decision is important, and considered response when the decision is complex. In the payroll case, for example, any delay caused by change evaluation may cost the responsible institution a great deal of money or trouble or both. On the other hand, a shoot-from-the-hip decision on the name-field-expansion question might also cost the institution dearly.

It is this dichotomy of functions that causes change evaluation to be a tricky concept to mesh into an organizational structure. The temptation is to name a change review board, place it tidily into a box solidly established in the organization chart, and assume that the problem is solved. In many cases, especially the complex ones where much deliberation is required, the problem may well be solved. But organizational hierarchies are notorious for being slow-moving. In those change evaluation cases where speedy consideration *is* needed, the calling and convening of a change board may well dangerously inhibit the change process. Acknowledging that problem, the best solution to the change evaluation process is probably still the change board, formally acknowledged on the organization chart. The charter defining the responsibilities and activities of that board, however, should clearly state an emergency decision process for those occasions when instant change is necessary.

Software maintenance changes may well have broad repercussions, reverberating throughout the responsible institution. Because of this, the change board should be placed very high in the software organizational structure and have representative membership from nonsoftware parts of the institutional organization, either as permanent members or on call for specific change decisions of applicability to them. For example, in the maintenance of an aircraft crew flight-training simulator, some changes could affect the organization which designs and builds the aircraft, and perhaps even the pilots and other crew members themselves. They, of course, must be represented in decisions involving that type of change; on the other hand, deciding to fix an internal software bug that does not affect the external world except to cause erroneous results is probably not of interest to them. In either case, however, the participation of top-level software managers in the change review process may be critical to the success of the change, particularly if high-priority computer time or organizational intercooperation is a factor in the change process.

Again, such top-level participation is not always desirable or necessary. The 2:00 A.M. call to the payroll maintenance programmer to fix a bug before the checks are run is a well-known software phenomenon! Top-level software managers are frequently and understandably not interested in participating in that kind of change review. Thus, the formal change review process should possess the previously mentioned escape clause by means of which emergency change authority is delegated to responsible subordinates. It may be difficult or impossible to spell out a definition of circumstances under which such changes may be made. An after-the-fact accountability to the change board for emergency changes may be the best solution to this dilemma.

All of this discussion has been oriented toward a very formal change review process. There are many instances, however, when such a formal process is neither necessary nor desirable. For example, in a very small software organization, or on a very small software project in a large organization, such formality is obviously out of touch with reality. Perhaps even more commonly, the existence of an especially highly capable and responsible maintenance programmer may obviate the need for formal change review. Thus, it is the intent of this section to promote the concept of change review, without specifically recommending a level of formality or even an organizational structure for that concept. As has previously been mentioned, it is the educated intuition of the manager that must ultimately be responsible for answering the hard-to-answer questions—including when to apply formality, and how much, and to whom.

4.2.2   Change Activity Review

An often-neglected part of the software maintenance process is the notion of tracking change activity. Whether the changes being made are fixes to errors or changes resulting from software product customer inputs, it is important to keep track of those changes. Which changes, for example, have actually been correctly made and tested and closed out? Which changes were made incorrectly and are being reworked? Which changes are temporary, until time for a better solution comes along? Which changes are still being evaluated? When are the changes expected to be completed? When were completed changes actually completed (or more to the point, what version of the software contains them)? What are the work-arounds for programmers or customers otherwise stalled by the changes? Are the changes increasing in volume or decreasing? (This is a window into the more important question of whether the software is getting better or worse.) Are the unfixed changes increasing in number or decreasing? (This is a window into the more important question of whether the maintenance staff is adequate for the volume of changes coming in.)

Most of these questions are answerable by the utilization of a fairly straightforward software change tracking system. The essence of such a system is two procedural considerations: the use of some sort of standardized change reporting form, such as a software problem report (SPR), which allows responsible people to note the nature of a problem, the nature of the solution to the problem, and the progress toward achieving that solution, all on the same form; and the preparation of change activity review or problem status reports, extracted from the current file of software change report forms, which answer the questions illustrated above. Examples of such forms and reports are given in figures 4.2.2-1 and 4.2.2-2. Further discussion of these topics occurs below and in ref. [7].

Not only is it important to report and track software problems, it is also important to know when to track, and for how long.

Typically, in the software life cycle, a great amount of error detection will occur before a formal tracking system is necessary. Errors discovered in the analysis and design phases, for example, are generally not tracked, since they are usually corrected in the emerging specification and design as they are discovered. Even during the code and checkout phase, errors are usually not tracked because they are too numerous and because the time to fix is often less than the time to report. It is after a software product begins acceptance testing, or is released to the customer, or begins system integration (preferably, whichever comes first) that a formal tracking system becomes necessary.

Figure 4.2.2-1 Suggested Software Problem Report Form

SOFTWARE PROBLEM REPORT

Problem Report No. _____

Project Name _____ Computer/Lab Utilized _____ Program _____

| **Problem Discovery** | Name of finder _____ Date _____ |

| **Method of detection**
□ Usage
□ Inspection/Analysis | □ Development test
□ Integration test
□ Acceptance test | **Tools used to detect**
□ None
□ Design review
□ Peer review | □ Dump (terminal)
□ Dump (dynamic)
□ HOL Debug
□ Analyzer | □ Simulation
□ Assertion
□ Proof
□ Other |

Description of symptoms _____

_____

_____

Configuration level _____

Correction importance/need date _____

Authorizing Signature _____ Orgn. _____ Date _____

| **Problem Analysis** | Name of analyst _____ Start date _____ End date _____ |

Findings _____

_____

Resources expended: person _____ computer _____

Estimated resources to correct: person _____ computer _____

Workaround _____

_____

| **Problem Correction** | Name of programer _____ Start date _____ End date _____ |

Description of Correction _____

_____

_____

Components changed and configuration level _____

Resources expended: person _____ computer _____

Problem category -
□ Job control language □ Operational Interface □ Coding error - data declaration □ Coding error - executable instruction	□ Design error - omitted logic □ Design error - faulty logic □ Testing □ Configuration management	□ Documentation □ Other □ User error

Final Authorizing Signature _____ Orgn. _____ Date _____

147

Figure 4.2.2-2 Sample Change Activity Review Reports

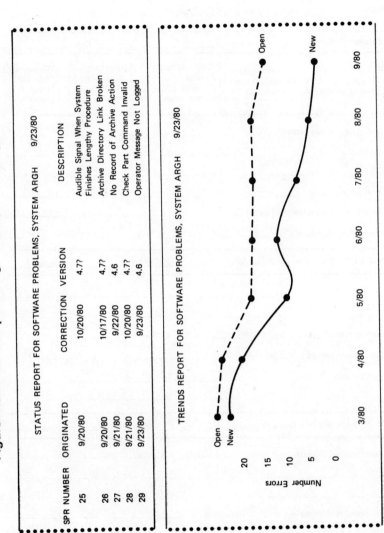

STATUS REPORT FOR SOFTWARE PROBLEMS, SYSTEM ARGH   9/23/80

SPR NUMBER	ORIGINATED	CORRECTION	VERSION	DESCRIPTION
25	9/20/80	10/20/80	4.7?	Audible Signal When System Finishes Lengthy Procedure
26	9/20/80	10/17/80	4.7?	Archive Directory Link Broken
27	9/21/80	9/22/80	4.6	No Record of Archive Action
28	9/21/80	10/20/80	4.7?	Check Part Command Invalid
29	9/23/80	9/23/80	4.6	Operator Message Not Logged

TRENDS REPORT FOR SOFTWARE PROBLEMS, SYSTEM ARGH   9/23/80

The organizational location of these change activity review processes is less important than their existence somewhere in the organization. In many cases, it is best provided by the maintenance programmer himself. However, on large or complex systems, especially those where a large team is responsible for maintenance activities, it may be better to have a separate group designated to provide the necessary support, especially in the preparation of reports from the file of software change forms.

4.2.2.1   PROBLEM REPORTS

Regardless of who does the work organizationally, whenever a software problem is discovered after the tracking system is initiated, an SPR must be filled out and a number assigned to it. The SPR should clearly state the problem symptoms, and be accompanied by physical evidence of the existence of the problem and sufficient information to allow its re-creation.

Types of errors that are reportable include:

1.   Software malfunction (self-contained or interfacing)
2.   Documentation error
3.   Software inefficiency
4.   Test case/procedure error

A priority for correction of the error should be established. The priority should take into account the generality of the problem (is it disabling? will it affect other usage?), the ability to work around it, the degree to which the originator himself is stopped by the occurrence, and the relative importance of the originator's work. The priority should be noted prominently on the SPR form.

The SPR, once filled out, should be given to the responsible software organization. The software maintainer should briefly examine the SPR to see if it may affect a program portion he is already working on and to determine its priority. The SPR should then be filed, pending its emerging to be worked in priority sequence.

When the SPR comes up for work, an analysis of the problem and determination of a probable correction is made. The result of this analysis is noted on the SPR form. The nature of the correction is then submitted to the change board.

Once change approval is received, the software correction is coded and inserted into the program. The updated code, perhaps including corrections to one or more other problems, is then executed against the specific test situations on which it failed. If it passes that test, the corrected software is then executed against a regression test to ensure that no problems have been created by the correction. If any of these tests fail, the correction must be redesigned and recoded and retested. If all tests succeed, the software is ready to be considered for release to its previous environment (acceptance test, usage, etc.). This process is illustrated from an organizational point of view in figure 4.2.2-3.

4.2.2.2   PROBLEM STATUS REPORT

Developers, users, and managers need to be kept aware of the status of specific problems as well as the general status of the software. To this end, a problem status report is needed.

The problem status report originates from the SPR file. It should cover at least the following, preferably by priority:

1. New problems reported, their nature, and their probable disposition.
2. Old open problems, their nature, and their probable correction date.
3. Problems closed since the last report, their nature, and the disposition.
4. Trends data—a graph showing the history of the count of open SPRs and the history of problem reporting frequency.

Via the problem status report, it should be possible to look up the status of any given problem, check to see if a problem you have encountered may already be on the list, and grasp the overall progress in removing errors from the software.

Most important in the problem status report process is the question of distribution of reports. Obviously, the reports provide valuable information for management, especially the ones that by implication answer the questions of whether the software is getting better or worse, and whether the manning level of the maintenance team is adequate. But equally important, the users of the software need the reports.

Figure 4.2.2-3 Example of SPR Processing Organizational Flow

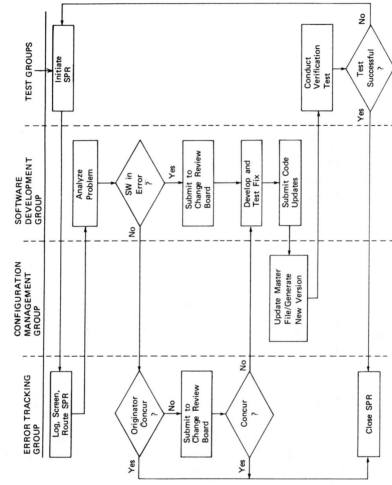

151

Work-around information is vital to users. So is an idea of when "their" particular change is likely to be completed. And so is an understanding of which versions of a piece of software contain which fixes.

Change activity review reports, in short, form a vital communications medium for both the manager and the troops. This often-neglected software maintenance activity is a vital part of linking the software maintainer into the world outside his maintenance realm.

4.2.3   Product Certification

There is a problem in software maintenance which even experienced managers and programmers find difficult to acknowledge. The installation of one software change all too frequently dislodges some previously-perfectly-correct piece of the same software. Thus, the maintenance activity is not simply one of providing the requested or required changes, but also one of guarding against causing more problems than you solve. Because of this fact, the role of certification of changed software is especially vital. Obviously, software changes must go through some sort of verification/validation process before the software is re-released to production use. But not so obviously, even the unchanged portions of the software must be subjected to that process.

Whether the test is for these so-called "regression errors" (those spawned by an unrelated change), or whether it is merely for the change itself, a test process is vital to the broader process of software maintenance. However, since such testing is also necessary for the product when it is first released, the verification/validation process is not unique to the maintenance process and therefore will not be discussed here in complete detail.

There are some parts of this process that *are* unique to maintenance. For one thing, during maintenance a body of test cases and other verification/validation processes already exists for the software, since it was built originally for the developmental and acceptance testing of the software. Maximum use of these cases and processes should be made during maintenance, both to eliminate the extra work of preparing new tests and to ensure that rigorous testing is applied to newly released maintenance software versions just as it was to the first release. These processes would, of course, include the use of performance analysis tests, to verify that the software still meets such constraints as sizing and timing, as well as the more reliability oriented tests, which determine whether the software does its job properly or not.

For another thing, consideration must be included for detecting the regression errors mentioned above. Largely, this is not a problem, since the original bundle of development test cases is presumably broad enough to test the software well beyond the scope of the current set of changes. But additionally, the standard set of tests should be augmented during maintenance to include tests specifically prepared to evaluate the most recent change. It is not at all uncommon to find that change $(n + 1)$ may unglue change n. Such special tests can pinpoint those problems.

Perhaps most important, the maintenance testing process is an iterative one. That is, the acceptance test must not be passed just once, as is true for the development process, but continually, each time a set of maintenance changes is installed. Therefore, it is important that the tests be easily run and their results easily analyzed.

Two principal techniques have been developed to aid in the process of test-case-result analysis. One is the software self-test. That is, the test case not only tests the software for errors, but internally detects those errors and provides a capability to report them. Such a technique is commonly used for test cases for a compiler, for example, where the test case is itself a program that is executed after the compilation process to see if it works, and where it fails.

The other test-case technique is the file comparator. Where the self-test is difficult or impossible to use, a practical alternative is the preparation of a permanent file of correct test-case results. Following a test run, the new results are compared against the old by an automated file comparator program (see section 3.2.1.1), either a general-purpose one more often used for source file comparisons, or a special-purpose one designed to isolate and highlight not only the failures but some explanation of possible causes of the failure based on what the test case intended to test.

The alert reader may well notice the similarity between the notion of product certification, as presented here, and the software development organizational concept sometimes referred to as "product test" [29, 35]. Actually, the two functions are nearly identical, with the development functions and responsibilities being a nearly comprehensive subset of the responsibilities of those of product certification. It would not be at all uncommon for the product certification maintenance activities to be a part of the product test organization, if one exists, and probably that is a desirable solution. On the other hand, for projects and organizations where there is no product test organization, product certification will probably happen in a manner analogous to the way product test was performed during development. As with the other concepts in this section, the importance lies in providing the function rather than with its placement in the organizational structure.

4.2.4   Configuration Management

The benefits and problems of configuration management are not all unique to the software maintenance activity. There is, however, an added complexity that must be dealt with here—that of version control.

As a software system undergoes change, repeated releases are made of the product, each with a new level of changes installed. In the best of all possible worlds, each new version would totally obsolete the old. As most of you already know, this is not the best of all possible worlds. (This was hinted at in section 3.2.1.1!) What in fact usually happens to contaminate or otherwise clutter the maintenance release problem is something like one of the following:

1.   The software product is used at a lot of different installations, from Podunk to Poughkeepsie. Not all new versions reach these installations at the same time, nor are they all implemented simultaneously, no matter how steadfastly the maintainer insists that they must be. As a result, the inevitable happens—a software error or change is reported in the context of an obsolete version of the system. The software maintainer may reluctantly be forced to replicate the problem or the change in an old version of the product. Configuration management is thus given the additional task of keeping a library of once-current versions of the software, probably with a set of matching documents and other product accoutrements. Obviously, this is not a desirable situation, and one which may call for management strength rather than technical responsiveness, but still in the inevitable case where

the problem must be dealt with technically the capability to do so must be provided.

2. The $(n + 1)$ software release solved a lot of problems, but it also regressed in one area, causing a problem that the n release did not have. While those customers affected are waiting for the $(n + 2)$ release to fix this calamity, they have to have some way to keep being productive. One solution may be to back up to some version of the system, hopefully n, which did indeed allow them to receive productive results. However, we now have in-house the very situation that was described in (1) for a multiinstallation dilemma. The solution, of course, is the same—more than one version must be maintained, and in fact in this case, more than one version must be currently active.

The result of this dilemma is that configuration management, for each product for which it is responsible, must keep not just one complete version of the software and its support material, but the equivalent of a pushdown stack of those things, one entry in the stack for each version of the product for which the software maintainers may still be held responsible. (Note that for this stack, access is not always to the most recently added item.) Again, the question of whether configuration management is a separate function organizationally, or one for which the maintainers must be responsible themselves, is less important than the functions that must be provided. All of the traditional configuration management practices employed for development activities [29, 31] must be employed for maintenance as well, but the concept broadens and deepens when the maintenance phase is reached. In fact, on many projects the configuration management function may not exist at all until the maintenance phase is begun.

An interesting discussion of an automated approach to this problem is found in ref. [10].

4.2.5   Possible Organizations

Emphasis has been placed throughout this section on the notion of providing functional capabilities rather than organizational structures. Obviously, different managers feel extremely strongly about different and sometimes conflicting organizational strategies. It is not at all uncommon to see one issue of a management journal extoll the virtues of a project-oriented organization, for example, and another issue make the same glowing claims for a functionally organized one. What is probably really happening is that different managers, because of their individual capabilities and style, are simply more comfortable and therefore more capable with different organizational strategies.

The purpose of this section, then, is to suggest ways in which the software maintenance activity can be amalgamated into a software organization. It is not the purpose of this section to identify a best way of doing so. Understanding that, figures 4.2.5-1 through 4.2.5-3 are provided.

Figure 4.2.5-1   The Timeshared People Organizational Structure: Software maintenance is performed by the same organization that performs software development. Often, in fact, the same people perform both roles.

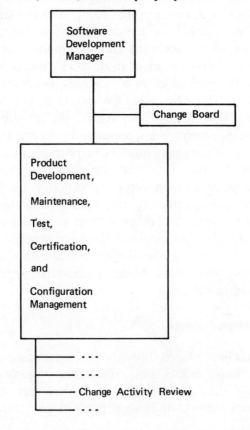

Figure 4.2.5-2   The Two-Headed Dragon Organization Structure: Software maintenance is performed in a second organization parallel to, but separate from software development.

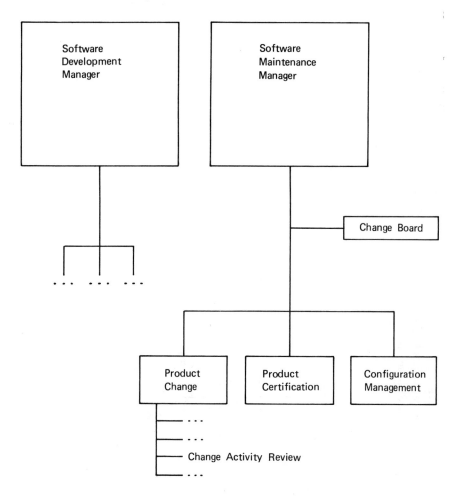

4.3   DOCUMENTING FOR MAINTENANCE

A curious phenomenon has occurred over the last several years in the field of software system documentation. "Good management methodology" has dictated that the internals or maintenance documentation of a program will be a complete set of English text

Figure 4.2.5-3 The Umbrella Organizational Structure: Software maintenance reports to the same manager as software development, but is performed in one or more separate organizations.

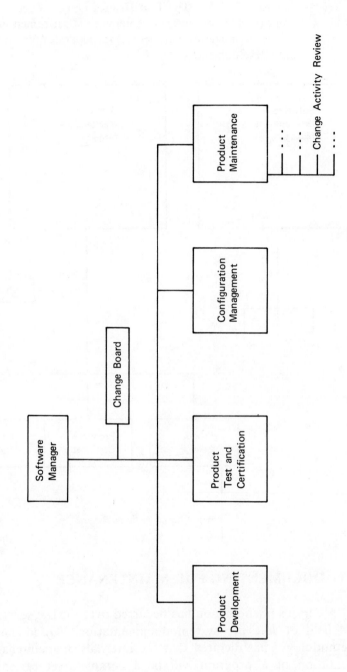

information bound together in volumes that for complex systems often reach several feet in width. The text information gives a system overview, explains each item and structure in the system's data base, shows control flow and data flow through the system, defines each major executable function, breaks down those functions into procedures, elaborates each procedure and its local data base, and cross-references both procedure calls and global data references.

All of that information is good information. The curious phenomenon is that placing this documentation in volumes separate from the program is *totally the wrong approach.* Documentation information about a software system belongs, in most cases, in the listing of the program itself. There are some key reasons for this; and there are some key reasons why we have veered so far in the wrong direction.

4.3.1   Why We Have Veered in the Wrong Direction

Programmers, in general, hate documentation. There seems to be something in the personality traits needed for the programming effort which precludes the ability to put together, or want to put together, words describing the programs produced.

This fundamental problem, which has been with us since programming became a profession in the 1950s, must underlie any discussion of documentation. Without the appropriate carrots and/or sticks, proper documentation will probably never come into being. This is true regardless, apparently, of how deeply the individual programmer believes in the philosophy of good documentation. Given a choice of nine other tasks to do, most programmers would put their documentation chore in tenth place on their personal pushdown stack. This underlying fact obviously precludes any naive arm-waving solutions to getting good documentation. Constant management attention is necessary to the achievement of adequate documentation.

There is another underlying factor that must also be dealt with. Computing managers, in general, hate the grubby-work of programming detail. One of the factors that motivates a technologist to move out of the programming world and into that of management is this dislike for detail. The manager, to be effective, must concentrate on a larger picture than assembly language instruction choices or high-order language statement types. This is an attractive lure to the battle-weary technologist tired of finding that his flags are uninitialized and his loops are badly nested. Unfortunately, the managerial need for focusing on the Big Picture pulls the manager slowly away from an ability to understand the end product that he or she is responsible for. Whatever the ways you choose to measure the elusive entity "quality of software"—and quality is often defined as a set of "ilities," such as maintainability, reliability, readability, and portability—it is almost impossible to evaluate the quality of a software product without poking around the innards of the software. And that means reading the listings.

But listing reading is the first chore that most managers reject when upward mobility snatches them from the world of the coding pad. And thus we have a built-in crisis situation—*those most responsible for the quality of software are those least able, by inclination and eventually by atrophied ability, to evaluate it.*

The ramifications of this problem are obviously profound in the software world. What is of interest in this section of this material, however, is the ramification of this problem on software documentation.

The intersection of these two problems—programmers hating documentation tasks, and managers hating code-reading tasks, is an inevitable bad compromise solution. Managers are, of course, responsible for the production of documentation, since programmers abdicate that responsibility. And managers would never consider, of course, placing the documentation in the program listing since by doing so they would be placing it out of their reach. The result is the current practice—program documentation is written in English text form, and placed in separate volumes.

4.3.2   What Is Wrong with Separate Documentation

There are two prime reasons for producing internals or maintenance documentation. The first and most important reason is to enable programmers responsible for a software system to understand it. The second, and rather unrelated reason, is as a control mechanism to be used at such times as preimplementation design reviews.

This discussion will concentrate on the former. The latter, although it is sometimes required at the detail level in some government and other software procurements, is obviously best satisfied by top-level design information elaborated only to the extent necessary to give the reviewers confidence that the designers have thought through the problems of the task in sufficient detail. The role of that top-level description in the overall domain of internals documentation will be returned to later.

The point was made above that internals documentation is written for programmers to make use of. This is an important point, since it distinguishes this kind of software documentation from most other kinds. User's manuals, for example, are meant to be read by users. Specifications are meant to be read by both customers (to give them the ability to determine that the problem being solved is the one they want solved) and designers. Test documents are meant to be read by customers (to determine that proper reliability techniques are being employed) and testers.

It is also true that, with the exception of the user's manual, internals manuals are the least transient and therefore among the most important of software documentation. Whereas specifications and test documents, for example, point to a specific event (requirements review, acceptance testing) and then become only matters of historic record, the internals manual (and the user's manual) must remain valid as long as the software system remains useful.

The target audience and the long-term value of the internals manual are too often forgotten in the rush to get the documentation produced and accepted. Worse yet, these factors are usually forgotten once the initial approval for the documentation is received.

The result is, and most programmers would support this alarming statement, that *most software internals documentation is inadequate to meet the needs of its target audience, and, worse yet, what is present is frequently out of date and thus unreliable.* Thus, our now traditional approach to this documentation is largely a failure.

4.3.3 What Is the Right Solution to This Dilemma?

What, in fact, do programmers responsible for revising a piece of software do? They go to the listing. This listing is, of necessity, accurate, since it is the program in all the real senses of the word. For the same reason, it is complete. Thus, the only accurate and current representation of a program, in today's technology, is frequently the program listing. It is this fact that forces the only reasonable solution to the problem of software internals documentation. Most of it must take the form of readable programs and commentary within the listing. With this solution, the explanations for a piece of software are placed with the encoded representation of the software. If the code is changed, it is much more likely that the documentation will be also (although it is still obviously not assured!). In addition, the explanations in the listing will be more likely to be readable by the intended target audience—a programmer. They will also be in the place where he needs most to find them. The accuracy and completeness attributes of the listing will also tend to apply as well to the documentation.

Some recent trends in modern programming technologies enhance this point of view. Structured programming, particularly in languages with adequate control structures where indentation systems can graphically assist in the understanding of the code, produces programs which at the logic level are sometimes self-documenting. (This should not, however, be taken to mean that the function and philosophy of the code are understandable without supplementary commentary.) In addition, languages and link-loaders, which permit the use of readable and self-defining names, take an even longer step toward self-documenting programming—DO VALIDITY TEST is a self-defining procedure name, for example, whereas DOVT is devoid of all but the most cryptic meaning. (Note, however, that it is easy to misuse the self-defining name facility, either by ignoring it out of laziness, or by imposing structured naming conventions to the detriment of the name's mnemonics. Note also that most contemporary link-loaders thwart this capability for externally referenced names, usually limiting programmers to the unfortunate Fortran-imposed de facto standard of six-character names.)

Be that as it may, the correct answer to the problem of internal documentation is heavy usage of the listing—lots of commentary, performing the same role as the now-traditional separate English text; good readable names; and graphically clear structure. At the detail level, the result will tend to be complete and accurate internals documentation.

It was mentioned previously that internals documentation also sometimes plays the role of a system overview for design review purposes. With the detail level of documentation now properly assigned to the listing, notice how clear it becomes that this stratum of documentation is, in fact, a separate breed of cat. Top-level documentation should occur as English text and probably even as a separately bound volume. With the distinction between top level and detail in better focus, we can now supplement the traditional role of internals documentation to include some previously lacking features—design decision information and underlying philosophic goals. In addition, a better link between the top level and lower levels can be made. The internals document can contain explanations for the role of, and pointers to, the middle-level software components, which tie together the top and detail levels.

The definition of good internals documentation has now evolved, from this discussion, into the following:

  I. Top-Level software definition (document, probably slim)
     a. Overall structure summary
     b. Overall data base summary
     c. Design decision data
     d. Underlying philosophy
     e. Midlevel structure(s)
     f. Midlevel data base(s)
     g. Pointers to detail-level information in the listing
 II. Detail-level software definition (listing)
     a. Commentary for
       1. Detail structure
       2. Detail data base
       3. Detail functions
       4. Implementation anomalies
     b. Readable names
     c. Structured, indented code

To be more specific, the categories listed above should include at least the following:

  I. Top-level definition
     a. Overall structure summary—words and pictures showing how the entire system hangs together. Probably a functional block diagram, showing major program

components, should be included. Better yet, the block diagram should be augmented to show (1) overlay structure, if any; (2) execution order; and (3) data flow. If this is not achievable in one diagram, then use several.

b.   Overall data-base summary—words and pictures showing the role of data in the total system. What are the major files, the major structures, the major clusters? How are they used, and where?

c.   Design decision data—this is the design history information, discussed in section 3.2.3.1. Often these are handwritten original notes, with a rudimentary index (if any) superimposed on them.

d.   Underlying philosophy—the most commonly omitted software documentation section. *Why* was the program designed the way it was? What programming style was used? What was the program really trying to achieve? Some programmers may be unaware that they have a philosophy. To the extent that they have and are aware of it, however, it is important documentation.

e.   Midlevel structure—given the overall structure of item a, what must the reader know to be able to go to the listing and understand the detail documentation found there? Answers to this question, which may be complex if the system is large, must be included here. After item d, this is the most commonly missing level of software documentation.

f.   Midlevel data base—analogous to item e, there must be a tie-in between the overall data base and the listing.

g.   Pointers to detail-level information—it is important to put detail-level information in the listing. It is also important to be able to find where in the listing certain information is. The top-level document should help the maintainer find his way around the listing. Where is procedure HOOPLA? Where is data structure FRAMMIS? Where is cluster CLOISTER?

II.   Detail-level definition

a.   Commentary—good commentary style was discussed in section 3.2.2.1.

b. Readable names—naming conventions were discussed in section 3.2.2.1.

c. Structured, indented code—program structure was discussed in section 3.2.2.1.

4.3.4   What Problems Remain?

All of this tidy-sounding discussion leaves one loose end dangling. Remember the two underlying facts, the programmer's hatred of documentation and the manager's hatred of detail? Putting detail documentation in the listing is not a solution to these problems; in fact, it makes the latter problem worse. Clearly, the software manager must still be responsible for achieving the production of internals documentation, and we have tucked it away in the last place he wants to look—the listing. However, there are two factors that mitigate these problems, which can eventually result in snipping the dangling loose ends. For one thing, programmers are much more likely to produce well-commented listings than separate documentation. Thus, the manager's motivational task is made easier. For another thing, inevitably managers must be able to read listings. It is as absurd for a first-line software manager to avoid listing reading as it would be for a first-line TV-manufacturing manager to avoid looking at the TV sets that he is responsible for. A manager must be able to inspect and understand the product he or she produces. The listing, in all the workable meanings of the word, *is* the software product.

Current managerial technology is management by remote symptom (as evidenced by concentrating on English-readable text material, which is not the product being produced and often fails to reflect the product accurately). This has, in fact, given rise in some technological circles to a kind of "double-entry bookkeeping" approach, where the English text describes the product the manager wants to believe is being built, and the listing describes the product as it is actually built. Under these circumstances, the notion of management control is a sham and a joke. If it is accepted that managers must be able to read listings, at least at the commentary level and probably beyond, then the last argument against detail documentation in the listing dissolves.

What is left, then, is some new forward motion toward something that many have discussed, but few have achieved—self-documenting software. Programmers can write it and rely on it, and managers (enhanced by some reborn skills) can control it and motivate it. But bear in mind that the top-level overview document is still vitally necessary—and to that extent the self-documenting goal is closer, but still out of reach.

4.4   ENVIRONMENT FOR MAINTENANCE

Your basic software maintenance person, unsung hero though he may be, is really the same kind of person as your software developer. Because of that, it may seem absurd at first thought to discuss special work environment considerations for the maintainer.

To some extent, it *is* absurd. Since software maintenance is a microcosm of the development world, the software maintainer needs the same kind of physical facilities as the software developer. If that means private offices at your installation, then the maintainer should have one, too. If that means team-sized cubicles, then maintainers should also be in cubicles. And if that means an acre or so of open bullpen, with upright bodies placed at desks stretching in rows as far as the eye can see, then so be it for the maintainer as well.

Except for one thing. The maintenance programmer has a unique need for storage space. He needs cabinets for back listings, bookcases for historic documentation, and perhaps even card or tape or disk pack files for physical back versions. The very fact of version iteration, as discussed earlier, means that the maintenance programmer is responsible for *n* versions of each active or inactive program that he is maintaining. Hopefully, *n* is small, but *n* seldom, if ever, reduces to 1.

Much of this storage requirement is the burden of the configuration management group. Typically, configuration management saves all back versions of a piece of software that were once significant, whether they are currently active or not. But even the software maintainer— assuming that maintenance and configuration management are performed by different groups—has special storage needs. Just the active versions of a piece of software will usually be enough to force special storage requirements for the software maintainer. It is often possible to spot the maintainers by the forest of tall cabinetry around their desks!

Although storage is the only truly unique environmental requirement of the maintainer, it would be a mistake to omit one other subject:

quiet. Remember that the maintainer is one who must innovate within constraints. The kind of mental exercise which that demands is best performed in an isolated atmosphere, undunned by the clatter of typewriters and the chatter of colleagues. Probably quiet is best obtained by setting aside an area of study carrels [14] where the programmer may go to think in peace. However, the requirement for access to historic materials may make that infeasible for the maintainer —carrying a wheelbarrow load of back listings and documents to a carrel is clumsy at best. Perhaps a quiet time of day for a particular work area is another solution. Oddly, neither of these solutions is commonplace. Except in the private office environment, quiet seems to have a low priority in the traditional manager's eyes. A poll of technologists, especially software maintainers, would result in a different priority entirely.

4.5 REFERENCES

1. "The Economics of Software Quality Assurance," Proceedings of 1976 National Computer Conference; Alberts.

    Analyzes the software life cycle from an economic point of view to determine when emphasis on quality assurance techniques should be placed. Examines the effectiveness of SWQA techniques and tools (structured programming, top-down development, chief programmer teams, automated tools). Concludes that SWQA emphasis should be on "the early detection and elimination of design errors."

2. "The Relation of Internal Communication to R&D Project Performance as a Function of the Nature of the Project," M.I.T. Industrial Liaison Program WP 1016, 1977; Allen, Lee, and Tushman.

    Studies the role of communication in enhancing project performance. Finds that different functions must be managed in different ways, depending on the nature of the tasks and the staff.

3. "Software Engineering," IEEE Transactions on Computers, December 1976; Boehm.

    Defines software engineering and constituent parts. Discusses costs and trends. Section VII, Software Maintenance, says that maintenance accounts for about 70% of the cost of software and is a "highly neglected activity."

4. "Modern Programming Practices Study Report," RADC-TR-77-106, 1977; Branning, Willson, Schaenzer, and Erickson.

Section 6 of this report describes the configuration management practices employed on four major programming efforts performed by Sperry Univac for the U.S. Navy. Evaluations of effectiveness are made.

5. *The Mythical Man-Month,* Addison-Wesley, 1975; Brooks.

A treasury of insights into software management, drawn from practical experience on the implementation of OS/360.

6. "Maintenance of the Computer Sciences Teleprocessing System," Proceedings of the International Conference on Reliable Software, 1975; Bucher.

Describes maintenance activities on a specific project. Stresses management of maintenance. Shows the role of the "change advisory board" and "system evolution conference." Discusses change records and testing techniques.

7. "A Communication-oriented Approach to Structuring the Software Maintenance Environment," Proceedings of the Ada Environment Workshop, November 1979; Cashman and Holt.

Describes a software-problem report tracking system called MONSTR, which facilitates communication among maintainers regarding software errors.

8. "Resource Analysis for Data-processing Software," General Research Corp., 1977; Dodson.

Investigates contemporary software costing practices. Suggests areas for further research.

9. "A Study of Fundamental Factors Underlying Software Maintenance Problems," ESD-TR-72-121, Vol. 11, 1971.

A series of interviews with programmers on maintenance-relevant subjects. Also contains maintenance programmer diaries and case study reports.

10. "Make—A Program for Maintaining Computer Programs," Software Practice and Experience, April 1979; Feldman.

Describes a configuration management tool that runs on the Unix operating system and assists in the rebuilding of complex software systems after parts of them are modified.

11.   "Software Acquisition Management Guidebook; Cost Estimation and Measurement," System Development Corp. report SDC-TM-5772/007/02, 1978; Finfer and Mish.

Provides a basic understanding of Air Force software cost estimation methodologies and reviews several models.

12.   "E-3A Software Maintenance," Proceedings of the AIAA Conference on Computers in Aerospace, 1977; Fox.

Describes maintenance activities on a DoD command and control project. Discusses the E-3A project itself, the management structure for software maintenance, and the activities involved.

13.   "Testing Maintainability," ACM SIGSOFT Software Engineering Notes, April 1979; Gelperin.

Suggests techniques oriented to evaluating software maintainability: standards auditing, "what if" analysis (to anticipate future change), structural evaluation (to better understand product cohesion and complexity), and production testing.

14.   "Environment and the Computer Programmer," PGR Quarterly Newsletter, Summer 1969; Glass.

Advocates team-oriented cubicles augmented by study carrels for quiet, and conference rooms for discussion, as an optimum environment for programmers.

15.   *Tales of Computing Folk: Hot Dogs and Mixed Nuts,* Computing Trends, 1978; Glass.

"Rusty Technology and Personal Oblivion" describes the dilemma of managers and technologists who have not kept up with the changing computing technology. "The Sky is Falling" describes the predicament of a manager unable to keep up with computing facility changes emerging from software enhancement requirements.

16.   "Lying to Management . . . a Legitimate Problem Solution?," *The Power of Peonage,* Computing Trends, 1979; Glass.

Chronicles the conflict between a skilled software maintainer and a technically unaware manager.

17.   *Software Reliability Guidebook,* Prentice-Hall, 1979; Glass.

Surveys techniques for achieving software reliability. Discusses the interrelationships among reliability, maintenance, and management.

Describes configuration management, quality assurance, and other organizational strategies.

18.   "MAIDS Study—Program Testing and Diagnosis Technology," Letter Report N7000-6-73, 1973; Goodenough and Eanes.

Discusses the inadequacy of testing and the importance of early detection of design errors. Includes regression testing in a general discussion of testing strategies.

19.   "A Perspective on Software Development," Proceeding of the 3rd International Conference on Software Engineering, 1978; Hetzel.

Describes the evolution of one manager's thinking on the problems of software development. Cites "ineffective management" as the largest causative factor, but observes that there is no one "main" problem.

20.   "Staffing the Albatross Project," Datamation, February 1976; Kenney.

A facetious look at the problems of staffing a tightly budgeted and scheduled project.

21.   "How Software Projects Are Really Managed," Datamation, January 1979; Lehman.

Summarizes the results of a comprehensive survey of largely aerospace oriented software managers regarding both technical and management practices used. Some results are nonintuitive (e.g., projects with no management control mechanisms fared better than average for on-time delivery!), whereas others are predictable (e.g., requirements should be clearly established before design, and design before programming). Mentions unusual practices (e.g., incentive pay, in-house competitive bidding on tasks).

22.   "Characteristics of Application Software Maintenance," UCLA Graduate School of Management, 1976; Lientz, Swanson, and Tompkins.

Surveys 69 computing installations to identify the characteristics of software maintenance. Studies largely COBOL-oriented environments with high ongoing maintenance needs.

23.   "Characteristics of Application Software Maintenance," Communications of the ACM, June 1978; Lientz, Swanson, and Tompkins.

An updating of ref. [22].

24.   "Scheduled Maintenance of Applications Software," Datamation, May 1973; Lindhorst.

Advocates "scheduled maintenance," where software changes are tracked and aggregated and installed all at once, as a management technique for minimizing maintenance staffing and production software perturbance.

25. "A Service Concept for Software Auditing," Proceedings of the NSF Software Auditing Workshop, 1976; Miller.

Advocates the Software Auditing Service, a quality assurance type of function that can be used to help achieve better software through audits. Types of audits and their potential cost are discussed via specifics. Includes a discussion of audit support tools.

26. MIL-STD-483 (USAF), Appendix VI, 1970.

Describes the detailed form and content requirements for military software specifications. The development (Part I) specification describes requirements; the product (Part II) specification describes the completed software's internal configuration.

27. "Research toward Ways of Improving Software Maintenance," ESD-TR-73-125, 1973; Overton, Colin, and Tillman.

Describes an experiment in which software maintenance activities were measured. Contains many quotes from maintenance programmers. Stresses the structure ("conceptual groupings") of the software. Defines specific maintainability techniques and a maintainability checklist. Discusses use of a graphics terminal to support maintenance.

28. "Automatic Software Test Drivers," Computer, April 1978; Panzl.

Discusses regression testing ("under present technology, effective regression testing is seldom possible") in the context of an automatic system for producing and retaining test procedures.

29. "An Investigation of Programming Practices in Selected Air Force Projects," RADC-TR-77-182, 1977; Perry and Willmorth.

Section II.4.4 is a frank discussion of organizational practices and failures in a large military project coded by System Development Corp. Results are quantified.

30. "A Systems Approach to Computer Programs," *A Management Guide to Computer Programming,* American Data Processing, 1968; Pokorney and Mitchell.

Elementary discussion of the role of computer programs in Air Force systems management. Defines the elements of the software development process and management participation in those elements. Cites examples, some painful.

31. "Implementing a Software Quality Assurance Program for the Viking Lander Flight Software," Transactions of Software 77 Conference; Prudhomme.

    Describes the Viking spacecraft and its mission to explore Mars. Gives a detailed description of the Viking SWQA program, which consisted of (1) design assurance, (2) configuration control, (3) verification/validation testing, and (4) failure reporting. Impacts on several Viking software functional areas are described.

32. "Viking Software Data," RADC-TR-77-168, "Software Change Request/Impact Summary," pp. 222–228, 1977.

    A frank discussion of the problems of change review on the Viking project. Includes forms and methodologies used.

33. "Some Comments on Comments," SIGDOC Newsletter, December 1976; Sachs.

    Ways of producing commentary to document a program are described. Structured programming and "self-documenting code" are dealt with frankly.

34. "The QA Role in Software Verification," Transactions of Software 77 Conference; Scholten.

    Stresses the total-life-cycle approach to software verification. Describes impacts of software quality assurance (SWQA) on each of those phases. Advocates a separate SWQA organization.

35. "An Organization for Successful Project Management," Proceedings of the 1972 Spring Joint Computer Conference; Smith.

    Presents a software project organization emphasizing separation of responsibilities and formal checks and balances. Defines the problems plaguing software development. Proposes a development group, an integration group, and a project test group, and discusses their roles.

36. "Software Acquisition Management Guidebook, Software Maintenance Volume," System Development Corp. TM-5772/004/02, November 1977; Stanfield and Skrukrud.

    Describes preventive maintenance techniques throughout the software life cycle. Specifically directed toward Department of Defense-procured software, but applies to all. Provides ideas and checklists for maintenance-oriented software review. Summarizes DoD regulations, specifications, and standards relevant to software maintenance.

37.   "The Dimensions of Maintenance," Proceedings of the 2nd International Conference on Software Engineering, 1976; Swanson.

Proposes to define theoretical bases of software maintenance. Defines corrective, adaptive, and perfective maintenance. Suggests the contents of a maintenance data base and a measure of maintenance performance. Recommends further research into the subject.

38.   "Error Data Collection in Software Systems," "Computer Software Reliability; Many State Markov Modeling Techniques," RADC-TR-169, 1975; Trivedi and Shooman.

Discusses the process of error reporting in the context of reliability modeling studies. Suggests improvements in current reporting techniques to assist the error modeler.

39.   *The Psychology of Computer Programming,* Van Nostrand Reinhold, 1971; Weinberg.

Discusses "egoless programming" and individual ownership of programs. Advocates the team approach to software development and reviews. Uses an anecdotal approach.

40.   "Program Standards Help Software Maintainability," 1978 Proceedings of the Annual Reliability and Maintainability Symposium; White.

Evaluates the impact of software standards on maintainability. Concludes that modularity, structured coding, and in-line commentary have merit.

Five

A Maintainer's Diary

One of the problems of textbook learning is that words and phrases can only simulate a small segment of the realities of a subject. It is one thing to talk about the importance of people in maintenance; to discuss the methodologies they can use; and to explore the problems and rewards of managing them. It is quite another thing to be handed the responsibility for maintaining a program: you are given a somewhat worn program listing, a stack of supporting documents alarmingly high (but not high enough, you will soon learn!), and pointed in the general direction of the computing facility.

As you browse the listing, concentrating heavily to understand the mind-sets of the programmer who preceded you, referring to the documents for support when necessary, the realities of maintenance finally hit you. This is hard, mind-taxing work; and as the months of your responsibility move by, you find that it continues to be a challenge, sometimes exasperating, sometimes depressing, and sometimes—when you finally find the bug that has eluded you for n weeks, where n is too large—euphoric.

This section of the book is an attempt to make that reality come a little bit alive. It is some excerpts from the diary of a real, live maintenance programmer. The diary is a slightly fictionalized account of a typical month. The time frame has been compressed and selected events have been expanded to provide the reader with a proper feeling for the environment.

The product being maintained is a high-order language (HOL) compiler in daily use in the development and maintenance of a large real-time system (containing more than 500 routines, totaling more than 50,000 statements, and employing more than 100 programmers). The events occur within a background of what is considered to be the "normal" maintenance activity, that is, correcting problems. The time intervals not described can be assumed to be filled with other occurrences similar to the ones mentioned.

THE MONTH BEGINS . . .

AUG. 1—8:21 A.M.
> A user is waiting at my desk with a listing when I arrive. He is new to the project and the language is new to him. He is attempting to use an assembly language routine to perform a function that exists as one of the features of the language. A short explanation of the existence of the feature and how to use it diverts him from assembly language.

AUG. 1—3:00 P.M.
> I submit all the compiler test cases for compilation and execution. A new compiler is being readied for release to the users, and this is the last function performed before making a compiler available.

AUG. 2—8-10 A.M.
> I pick up the test-case execution and analyze the output. The runs are all okay, finally. In the last week they have been run three times. The analysis previously had turned up minor problems, and changes had been inserted to correct those errors. This process would have been speeded up considerably with the use of a comparator.

AUG. 2—12-1 P.M.
> I prepare the release memo, which informs the users of the existence of a new version of the compiler and documents the changes that have been incorporated. The problems that are closed, annotated with the problem discoverer's name, changes in the use of the compiler, and new enhancements are all listed.

AUG. 2—4:00 P.M.

I submit the job which will copy the compiler to the file normally accessed by users to obtain the compiler. With the exception of those things noted in the release memo, the new compiler should be transparent to all users.

AUG. 4

The new version of the compiler is available. The release memo is sent out. All changes to the new version are documented, and the maintenance document and user's manual are updated.

AUG. 8—10:41 A.M.

A user comes in with question. The user's manual is pulled out, and the answer looked up. The description is somewhat vague. Further reference to the computer program listing gives the user his answer, but leaves me writing a problem report, checking the language specification, and rewriting a paragraph in the user's manual.

AUG. 9—4:42 P.M.

A user arrives with a big stack of listings. He says that he recompiled his program with the new version of the compiler and that it no longer does what it did with the old compiler.

(Maintainer to self: "Stay calm. It may not be a regression problem. You were pretty careful with that last set of changes. You ran all the tests and they looked okay.")

To user: "What is going wrong? Can you isolate the differences in the two runs?"

"Oh yes! This statement doesn't look like it's working."

Looking at the code generated by the compiler, I find that the wrong register appears to be being used. I pull out the code generator listing and turn to the section containing the offending code. Sure enough, right in the middle of the page is a correction that is in the newly released compiler. Close inspection of the compiler's code reveals a coding error—an uninitialized variable has been used. The original test had worked properly probably because the variable had contained a reasonable bad value, whereas in this compilation an unreasonable bad value had caused bad code to be generated. I provide a temporary work around for the user and file a problem report.

AUG. 10—10:25 A.M.

A user arrives with a listing. He says "my program blew up and I can't figure out what is going on." (What this really means is "I can't read a dump.") As I go through the dump-reading magic, I explain the things I'm doing. Eventually, we determine that a bad subscript value is being used and the user departs to correct his error.

AUG. 11—10:30 A.M.

A user shows up with a listing. The compiler is generating bad code. A problem report describing the problem is created, and a low priority is assigned to the problem. I identify the listing as to problem report number and file it; then I figure out a way for the user to work around the problem. The workaround is added, as a note, to the problem report. The report is filed.

AUG. 16—9:02 A.M.

A user asks: "What is the impact of increasing the region size with regard to the execution time for the compiler?" An explanation is given of the effects of increasing the region size (which is to decrease the execution time of the compiler).

AUG. 16—11:14 A.M.

A phone call is received from a remote site which is also using the compiler. About 20 minutes is spent verifying that a problem does indeed exist, asking questions, and directing the caller (remotely) to look for certain information. It sounds like a real problem. A problem report is written, and the user is asked to send a listing for further analysis.

AUG. 17—6:15 A.M.

I have come in early to work on a problem that requires some concerted effort with few interruptions. One of the new programmers asks where the light switches are. I give him directions to the panel box, and the rest of the area is bathed in light. (The software maintainer plays an indeed complex role in overall project goals!)

AUG. 18—10:30 A.M.

A user arrives with a dump. She has no object listing of the program. It is a typical example: the program blew up. "Can you figure out why?" she asks. Examination of the dump shows a call to a routine with a bad value for the address. Because the address is one that I know should have been resolved by the linkage editor, but instead contains a zero, and because some variations in the operating system have been installed and particularly because the linkage editor has had some trouble in the last week, I suggested recompiling with an object list, hoping the problem may not reoccur.

AUG. 19—8:21 A.M.

I walk to the computer room to pick up jobs that were submitted last night. The programmer with the dump yesterday is there and she mentions that she has recompiled and reexecuted the program and that apparently it worked okay. That reinforces my opinion that the linkage editor was probably bad. I tell her to come back if the problem reoccurs.

AUG. 22—2:45 P.M.

One of the users comes in with a listing and says that he has thought of a possible code improvement. He shows us the piece of code and suggests an alternative way of doing it which will save 30 to 40% of the time it currently takes. I write a note expanding on the idea and add a few wrinkles of my own, and file it in a book which I keep for that purpose. Improvements to code sequences are extremely beneficial when one considers that more than 500 object programs with a total of more than 50,000 statements are compiled. Small compiler changes can have a large impact on total system performance, particularly since they are executed in a real-time environment.

AUG. 23—8-12 A.M.

I continue to design and develop new areas of code, mostly in response to problem reports. When an area of code is modified for any reason, it is necessary and worthwhile to look at all the ramifications of the change. A constant goal is to improve the source so that later changes are unnecessary, or at least easier. The maintainer must again be thinking about the "next guy."

AUG. 24

As usual (when not working on something else), I have taken an open problem report and its associated listing and worked on it. A test case is generated. It is run against the old version and the test fails in the same manner as reported. The problem is found in the compiler modules. New code is written and that module recompiled. A test version of the new compiler is generated and when the test is run, the problem no longer occurs.

AUG. 29

A project with more than 100 programmers will experience turnover. As new programmers are brought onto the project, I give them a short training course (40 hours) in the use of the compiler, the computer's characteristics, and the philosophy of the project. This training is subtly extended by my presence; I also function in a consulting role. Programmers using the HOL often experience difficulties in its use. This is due to a variety of reasons: Experience with different dialects or implementations of the same language, lack of good programming background, the existence of compiler errors, proficiency in the use of a more powerful language, lack of certain background knowledge about the project, the sheer size of the project (which makes understanding a particular area difficult), idiosyncrasies of the host and target machines and their operating systems, and so on.

AUG. 29—4:00 P.M.

I prepare for tomorrow's class: looking over material to be presented, looking up answers to questions that could not be handled in class.

AUG. 30—8-12 A.M.

Class. No fixes, no enhancements will happen today. Today I am a teacher.

THE MONTH ENDS . . .

Conclusion: The maintainer is an active and integral part of a project's environment. He performs a variety of not-always-related services, ranging from fixing things to consultation to training and even to finding light switches! But the real meat of maintenance is found in the continuation of life for an existing program.

Six

Epilogue

This guidebook began with a pop quiz. You, the reader, were asked to answer a few apparently straightforward questions about software maintenance. The answers, you may recall, were not so straightforward. There are stereotypes and misconceptions loose in the software world, we saw, which have perverted the picture of software maintenance.

As this book explored those stereotypes further, a few truths began to emerge:

1. Software maintenance is much more than error correction.
2. Software maintenance activities are a microcosm of the whole software life cycle.
3. A lot of money is poured into software maintenance.
4. To be done properly, software maintenance should be a conscious goal from the very beginning of the software development process.

Working with those truths, it is then possible to achieve a more in-depth understanding of software maintenance.

We have explored, for instance, the role of people in the software maintenance field, the unsung heroes who keep the software machinery humming. We have seen that the *good* software maintainer must be flexible, broadly based, patient, self-motivated, responsible, and have a whole lot of other traits that cry out for capable, bright and experienced maintainers, not the junior or lowest-rated people we typically end up with. We have seen that the poorly understood concept of software style has a major impact on software maintenance through the problem of style clashes.

Given a better understanding of the people world of maintenance, we then explored the technology of maintenance. We have seen that the maintainer's toolbox is not bare, but neither is it well supplied. We have seen that the compiler is the focal tool of maintenance activities, leading to the concept of a more complete toolbox called the "supercompiler." We have seen that the best way to maintain software is to start with maintainable software, using a set of techniques called (not very satisfactorily) "preventing maintenance."

Then we explored the management of maintenance—the importance of people and the notion of people-sensitive management, the importance of reviews and audits to better understand and direct the maintenance process, and the role of change control and tracking in the overall maintenance process. And, somewhat shockingly, we exposed the authors' view that documentation for software maintenance has veered in totally the wrong direction, and explicitly discussed what should be done to get documentation back on the track.

Finally, we introduced a dash of reality into the otherwise textbookian discussion of maintenance. We browsed through a maintainer's diary, noting that maintainers not only fix things and interact with computers, but also consult with users, train customers, and even locate light switches! The maintainer's work, we were warned early, is never done.

Where, then, does software maintenance stand? It's a field with far too little said about it in the literature. It's a field with practitioners who are far too unaware of their own importance, as well as better ways of doing their job. It's a field with management equally unaware and inattentive.

All of that cries out for change. The front end of the software life cycle has gotten enormous attention over the past decade and a half. High-order programming languages begat high-order design languages which are begetting high-order requirements languages. Those languages are just a symptom of the new technology that is buzzing around the life-cycle front end.

That same kind of attention must also be focused on the software life cycle back end. Looked at both practically and economically, the life-cycle back end is where the action has to be. By far the most dollars and people resources are spent there.

This guidebook and its companion, *Software Reliability Guidebook,* attempt to provide a beginning of that focus. Hopefully, they will not be the ending. The back end of the software life cycle needs to be explored with the same kind of theoretical and pragmatic fervor as the front end. Hopefully, the next-generation *Software Maintenance Guidebook* and *Software Reliability Guidebook* will have a lot more to say than these!

Meanwhile, if you have software to maintain *now,* we hope we have helped!

—Robert L. Glass
Ronald A. Noiseux

Seven

Bibliography

A quick survey of the literature on software maintenance reveals some interesting facts;

1. It doesn't take long to survey, because not much has been written on the subject.
2. What has been written tends to focus on maintenance management rather than maintenance technology.
3. Maintenance and maintainers are called a lot of interesting things—"the tip of an iceberg" serviced by "unsung heroes" is one unlikely descriptor pair (not from the same paper).
4. Most of what has been written looks at military software maintenance, although there is a scattering of papers on commercial applications and system software.

The main bibliography of this book is found in the form of references attached to individual chapters. Many references are cited, but it will be noted by the astute reader that most of them are written for a purpose other than software maintenance and are relevant here by implication rather than by direct intent.

What follows are a selected few references that are either so important or so relevant that software-skilled people concerned about maintenance should be particularly aware of them.

The Mythical Man-Month, Addison-Wesley, 1975; Brooks.

"A Study of Fundamental Factors Underlying Software Maintenance Problems," ESD-TR-72-121, Vol. 11, 1971.

Special Collection on Software Science, IEEE Transactions on Software Engineering, March 1979.

The Elements of Programming Style, McGraw-Hill, 1978; Kernighan and Plauger.

"How Software Projects Are Really Managed," Datamation, January 1979; Lehman.

"Characteristics of Application Software Maintenance," Communications of the ACM, June 1978; Lientz, Swanson, and Tompkins.

"Requirements for Ada Programming Support Environments," February 1980, "Stoneman."

"Software Acquisition Management Guidebook, Software Maintenance Volume," System Development Corporation TM-5772/004/02, November 1977; Stanfield and Skrukrud.

The Psychology of Computer Programming, Van Nostrand Reinhold, 1971; Weinberg.

Index

189